C000039643

BOOM!

IGNITING THE POWER OF GOD'S WORD IN YOUNG PEOPLE'S LIVES

Copyright © 2012 Scripture Union
First published 2012

ISBN 978 1 84427 694 3

Scripture Union
207–209 Queensway, Bletchley, Milton Keynes, MK2 2EB
Email: info@scriptureunion.org.uk
Website: www.scriptureunion.org.uk

All rights reserved. No part of this publication may be
reproduced, stored in a retrieval system, or transmitted
in any form or by any means, electronic, mechanical,
photocopying, recording or otherwise, without the prior
permission of Scripture Union.

British Library Cataloguing-in-Publication Data
A catalogue record for this book is available from the
British Library.

Content adapted from *theGrid*
Additional material by Alex Taylor
Design by Phil Grundy
Printed by Melita Press, Malta

Scripture Union is an international Christian charity working
with churches in more than 130 countries.

Thank you for purchasing this book. Any profits from this book support
SU in England and Wales to bring the good news of Jesus Christ to
children, young people and families and to enable them to meet God
through the Bible and prayer.

Find out more about our work and how you can get involved at:
www.scriptureunion.org.uk (England and Wales)
www.suscotland.org.uk (Scotland)
www.suni.org (Northern Ireland)
www.scriptureunion.org (USA)
www.su.org.au (Australia)

Contents

Introduction

THE BIBLE IS A LIFE-CHANGING BOOK. THE STORIES WITHIN ITS PAGES TELL OF GOD'S GREAT PLAN FOR SALVATION. THEY ARE STORIES OF LOVE, GRACE, TRUTH, WONDER AND LIGHT. READING AND LISTENING TO THE BIBLE CAN TURN YOUR WORLD UPSIDE-DOWN!

If this is the case, why do we often shy away from opening up the Bible with young people, particularly young people with little or no church background? We can work with the assumption that young people, especially those who have not grown up in a church community, find the Bible boring and irrelevant. We fear that they will switch off if we get the big book out, that we will turn them off from the gospel.

Sometimes it is easier to go for sessions that look more at moral teaching, backed up with a couple of Bible verses, rather than helping young people engage with passages of the Bible. It's true that sessions like these get points across easily and introduce the Bible to young people who may never have encountered it before. However, the Bible has explosive potential: are we not in danger of turning such rocket-fuel-potential into the transformative power of a sparkler?

Boom! gives you the chance to try a different style with young people, including those with little or no church background. The activities here help you let young people loose on these Bible stories. How would someone who has never heard the story of Joseph react to it? What effect might the story of the prodigal son have on someone who has never encountered it before?

But if we let young people loose on the powerful stories of the Bible, what challenges would this mean for us? Well, we won't always finish up where we'd planned to – letting Scripture breathe and allowing God to speak means that we have to be ready for a number of different outcomes, as well as the one we are aiming for. We also have to be ready for many different questions.

However, letting Scripture breathe like this helps the Spirit do his work in our young people, guiding them to profound revelations about God, his love for us and what he did through Jesus. And this can lead to lives being transformed as young people meet with God.

BOOM. WHAT AN EXPLOSIVE PROSPECT.

How to use Boom!

THERE ARE 60 SESSIONS IN BOOM!, WHICH DIVIDE INTO 12 SERIES. THEY ARE ARRANGED IN BIBLICAL ORDER TO SHOW THE BIG STORY OF GOD'S SALVATION PLAN FOR THE WORLD, FROM CREATION TO JESUS' RETURN. YOU COULD START AT THE BEGINNING AND GO THROUGH THE WHOLE BOOK IN ORDER, OR YOU MAY PREFER TO PICK OUT PARTICULAR SERIES OR SESSIONS THAT ARE APPROPRIATE FOR YOUR GROUP AT DIFFERENT TIMES.

For each session:

- Begin by reading the Bible passage for yourself and think about how it relates to your group of young people. How might they react to it? What questions might they ask?

- Read through the *Boom!* activity and think about how it would work in your setting. Do you have all the equipment you need? How could you adapt it to better suit your group?

- If you are going to use the *Boom!* activity as part of a longer session, plan some games or other activities to do at the beginning and/or end of the session. It may be possible to link these to the theme of the Bible activity. (See *Ultimate Games* for ideas.)

- If you want to create a complete session based around the Bible passage, visit www.LightLive.org to find introductory and concluding activities for every *Boom!* session. You will need to register first, and then go to the 'Search LightLive' tab to search for the Bible passage. Filter by age to find activities suited to your group.

- Plan your session, checking that you have all the equipment and resources that you need. Make sure that you and your other leaders/helpers know what your roles and responsibilities are for the session.

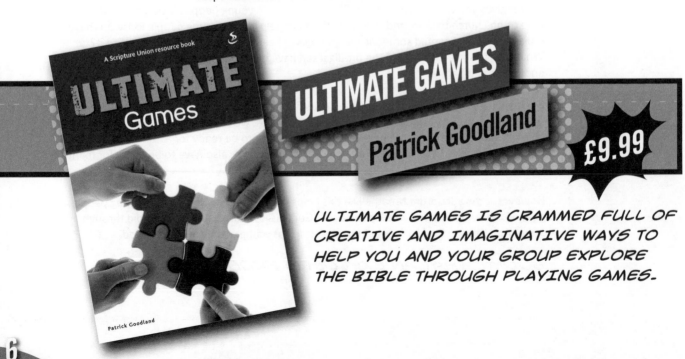

A Scripture Union resource book

ULTIMATE Games

ULTIMATE GAMES

Patrick Goodland

£9.99

ULTIMATE GAMES IS CRAMMED FULL OF CREATIVE AND IMAGINATIVE WAYS TO HELP YOU AND YOUR GROUP EXPLORE THE BIBLE THROUGH PLAYING GAMES.

Creation

CREATION CAN BE AN EMOTIVE SUBJECT, PARTICULARLY IF YOU GET ONTO THE SUBJECT OF THE BIG BANG ETC. BUT THE BEGINNING OF GENESIS DOESN'T SEEK TO PROVE TO US HOW GOD CREATED THE UNIVERSE, RATHER THAT HE DID. THE STORY HERE IS OF A GOD WHO BRINGS SOMETHING FROM NOTHING, ORDER FROM CHAOS, LIFE FROM DUST. HE IS THE ONE WITH THE POWER TO BRING SUCH COMPLEXITY INTO BEING WITH A WORD. GENESIS CHAPTER 1 SHOWS SUCH POETRY AND STRUCTURE THAT WE CAN'T FAIL TO SEE THE GOD BEHIND THE ACTION.

These chapters of Genesis are also the opening to the great narrative of the Bible, which culminates in Jesus' defeat of death and our reconciliation with God. Be sure to point this out to your young people. You might want to use some kind of timeline to help the young people place this part of God's great plan for salvation at the start of the Bible. This will help them build a picture of God's love for us and of the work God has done, and is still doing.

FOR THOSE FROM OUTSIDE A CHURCH COMMUNITY

Various aspects of the creation narrative are part of our culture – the concept of a day of rest, phrases such as 'In the beginning' – but young people who have not grown up in church may have no idea that these come from Genesis 1 and 2. There may be the desire to talk more about how the universe was created, but try to focus more on what these passages tell us about God: if God made the world, what does that tell us about his character? And about his attitude towards us?

Being made in God's image (Genesis 1:26,27) may be surprising to many, particularly those who suffer from low self-esteem. Be sensitive when talking about issues around this – you may want to open up other passages, such as Psalm 139, to help explore this idea further.

FOR THOSE WITH A CHURCH BACKGROUND

Young people who have grown up in church will undoubtably have heard the creation narrative before. They will probably have done many a craft around the creatures God created! In this case, familiarity may well have bred contempt, and this narrative may have lost much of its power and meaning, through the many retellings they have heard. You will need to find ways of coming at these passages afresh. The activity on Psalm 104 may well help you do this, as you can encounter God's love and creative power in a different way.

Church young people may, of course, suffer with issues of low self-esteem too, so be ready to sensitively discuss this.

IN THE BEGINNING

GENESIS
1:1–19

WHAT: *Reflective imaginary exercise*
WHY: *To discover more about our Creator God and to explore our response to him*
WITH: *A darkened room*

1 Explain to the group that you are going to take them on an imaginary journey. To help this, try to darken the room as much as possible and ask the group to close their eyes.

2 Say: Imagine you are in the cinema, waiting for a film to begin. It's a film you've been looking forward to seeing for ages. Imagine that you are the director/creator of this film. How do you feel? What are you thinking about? What type of film would it be? What characters would you have? What would you have them do? Now imagine what the opening scene is going to be. Imagine the way it comes into view; imagine what it looks like. What feelings does it inspire?

3 Raise the lights and explain to the group that the imaginary exercise is over and perhaps one day they will create their own movie but until then... Tell them that you are going to do another imaginary exercise but this time they are not the director. Darken the room again and ask them to close their eyes.

4 Read **Genesis 1:1–19** slowly, pausing between each phrase to let the group imagine the events as they unfold. Raise the lights and ask the group how the exercise made them feel. Has it made them think about the beginning of the world in a different way? Darken the room again and ask them to remember what they imagined. Read **Colossians 1:15–20**.

5 Raise the lights and ask whether the last passage made them change their imagined view of creation. Ask them who created the universe. What does the creation story tell them about God? Has it changed their opinion of him in any way? Invite some brief feedback.

MADE IN HIS IMAGE

GENESIS
1:20–31

WHAT: *Drawing and Bible study*
WHY: *To discover more about our Creator God and to explore our response to him*
WITH: *Bibles, felt-tip pens, paper*

1 Give out the felt-tip pens and paper and ask the young people to draw their favourite animal. When everyone has finished, compare the pictures and read **Genesis 1:20–25**. Chat for a while about why everyone chose that particular animal to draw – what is it about them that they like?

2 Then go on to chat about the differences between animals and people. Let the group decide on some characteristics and then read **Genesis 1:26–31**. List some of the things that these verses say about humans. The list might include: created in God's image, male and female, in charge of everything on the earth. In the opinion of the group, which is the most important thing on the list?

3 Ask the group why they think humans were the last thing God created. Why did God say everything was very good? What does it mean to be made in God's image?

BLESSED AND HOLY

GENESIS 2:1–3

3

WHAT: *Drama and discussion*
WHY: *To discover more about our Creator God and to explore our response to him*
WITH: *Copies of 'Busy, busy, busy' script from page 10, Bibles*

1 Ask for two volunteers to read or act out the 'Busy, busy, busy' script.

2 What is the group's reaction to the story? Does anyone think any of the things Ron was doing were 'wrong' or 'bad' things to do? Get some feedback on the nature of Ron's weekend. Does anyone else have weekends that are this busy?

3 Read **Genesis 2:1–3** to the group. Remind everyone what has happened so far in Genesis. As far as possible, get the group to fill in all the details they can remember. Explain that in the past people have always observed a day of rest because of this passage (and others in the Bible). What does the group think of the concept of a day of rest?

4 Talk a little bit about how God made us and how we need to take time out from our busy lives to rest.

PRAISE THE LORD!

PSALM 104

4

WHAT: *Creative reflection*
WHY: *To wonder at God's astounding creation*
WITH: *Art materials, pens, paper, modeling clay*

1 Set up your art materials around the room. Invite the group to choose a way in which to be creative during the Bible reading. Invite them to use whatever materials you have.

2 Ask a strong reader to read Psalm 104 or read it yourself (this would a good role to give someone who is not particularly creative). Challenge the young people to listen carefully to the psalm and make a representation of what they have heard.

3 Give the group time to finish their creations, and ask them to explain what they have made and why they made it.

4 Ask the group the following questions:

How would you describe the difference between what you've made and the real thing?
Have you ever looked at the world you live in and then wanted to praise God, like the psalmist?

5 Discuss what features of the natural world the group would include if they were creating the biggest global party ever. What would make the perfect setting for this party? The mountain ranges as the dance floor?

6 Another way of approaching this is to respond in mime or dance to the words being read. This is particularly good if you have a group that enjoys movement.

Busy Busy Busy

DON

HEY RON! WHAT ARE YOU UP TO AT THE WEEKEND? WANT TO COME ROUND MY HOUSE AND HANG OUT ON SUNDAY?

RON

I CAN'T, MATE, SORRY. IN THE MORNING I'M GOING TO CHURCH — I'VE GOT TO HELP WITH THE PA AND THEN GO TO YOUTH GROUP, THEN GIVE MY MUM A HAND WITH THE COFFEE AFTERWARDS. THEN WE'RE REHEARSING FOR A SKETCH WE'RE DOING IN NEXT WEEK'S SERVICE. THEN, AFTER LUNCH, I'VE GOT TO DO MY MATHS HOMEWORK. AFTER THAT I'M GOING TO MY GRAN'S TO MOW HER LAWN AND CATALOGUE HER HUGE COLLECTION OF BUS TICKETS — SHE'S GOT SOME THAT DATE BACK TO 1968! AFTER DINNER I'M GOING BACK TO CHURCH, WHERE THE YOUTH GROUP IS LEADING THE WORSHIP — I PLAY THE DRUMS AND THE UKULELE. THEN WE'RE HEADING OFF TO THE LOCAL HOMELESS SHELTER TO MAKE SOUP AND STEW FOR THE PEOPLE WHO NEED IT. AND I'VE GOT TO SQUEEZE IN MY ART HOMEWORK TOO — A LIFE-SIZE PICTURE OF CLIFF RICHARD!

DON

WHAT ABOUT SATURDAY?

RON

NO, I'M SOLVING WORLD HUNGER THAT DAY. SEE YOU LATER.

Fall, flood and promise

THIS SECTION CONTAINS SOME DIFFICULT STORIES, BUT DON'T BE PUT OFF BY THAT! THE STORIES OF THE FALL, NOAH AND GOD'S CALL TO SACRIFICE ISAAC ARE DIFFICULT EVEN FOR MATURE CHRISTIANS TO UNDERSTAND, BUT THAT DOESN'T MEAN THAT YOUNG PEOPLE WITH NO CHURCH BACKGROUND CAN'T WRESTLE WITH THEM AND DISCOVER MORE ABOUT GOD AND OUR RELATIONSHIP WITH HIM.

Helping young people understand the fall (Genesis 3) is important, to give them a bigger picture of what God is doing in the Bible. Jesus' actions on the cross are a direct response to man's disobedience and God's love for his people.

Although these stories are difficult, they tell us strongly of a God who cares for his people, who keeps his promises and who still wants a relationship with us, even though we often turn against him. Even though our stories are unlikely to be as dramatic as Adam and Eve, Noah or Abraham, God's attitudes still apply to us.

FOR THOSE FROM OUTSIDE A CHURCH COMMUNITY

The Bible passages covered here will bring up questions of God's judgement – young people may well demand to know how his actions are fair towards Adam and Eve, towards the people who die when Noah is safe on the ark, towards Abraham and Isaac. Use these questions as starting points for discussion about God's holiness and judgement – how different is God's way of living from that of today's culture? Also focus on God's faithfulness to Adam and Eve (even though they had turned against him), Noah and Abraham.

FOR THOSE WITH A CHURCH BACKGROUND

Like creation, these stories are often covered in children's groups in churches and so young people from a church background may well have encountered these before. Help these young people to see the place of these narratives in God's great plan for salvation through the Bible so that they can build up their understanding of what Jesus came to do.

APPLE DISASTER

GENESIS 3

WHAT: *Advertising discussion*
WHY: *To examine why we should do what God says*
WITH: *Bibles, selection of magazines or TV adverts, CD or MP3 player, audio version of the Bible*

1 Show the group a selection of adverts from magazines or TV. Ask them if they can spot different ways that advertisers try to sell their products. What does the advert promise? How might the reality be different?

2 Listen to **Genesis 3** from an audio version of the Bible or use *The Street Bible* by Rob Lacey. Divide the young people into groups of three or four and invite them to read the passage again.

3 Ask them to answer the following questions:
   • What did that fruit promise?
   • What did it deliver?
   • What went wrong?
   • What would be different in the world today if Adam and Eve hadn't given in to temptation?
   • Why is it important for us to do what God says? (Because he is God, he is the One, not us; because otherwise someone, somewhere gets hurt; because it's a good way of showing how much we love and respect him.)

4 Gather feedback from the groups.

5 Have a time of quiet and ask the young people to think again about why it is important for us to do what God says.

SAVING GRACE

GENESIS
6:9 – 8:19

WHAT: *Demonstration*
WHY: *To discover more of God's grace*
WITH: *Plastic globe or map of the world covered with plastic laminate, a water-soluble marker pen, water, cloth, DVD of* The Lord of the Rings: The Two Towers, *TV and DVD player or laptop and projector*

1 Invite the young people to suggest actions that are really bad. For each sin, invite someone to draw a blot on the globe or map.

2 Ask the group to suggest how to get it clean again. They should suggest using water! As you prepare the equipment, explain that this is a popular story to tell children because it has lots of animals in it and a nice boat. But, actually, it's a horrific story, showing us how much it matters to God when we do wrong stuff.

3 Tell the story of the flood, using the following key points (prepared from **Genesis 6:9 – 8:19** beforehand):

People were doing terrible things that made God wish he'd never made them. He decided to clean up the earth.

Because he is a God of grace, he found one good person, Noah, and saved the world through him. God told Noah to build a boat and to bring on board his family and two of every kind of animal so that the whole of creation had a second chance.

God sent a great flood that wiped out every living thing, except what was on the boat. (Wipe the blots off the world map here.)

Things were so bad on earth, that only a really drastic solution would do.

4 Show the scene from near the end of *The Two Towers* where the Ents march on Saruman's tower and 'cleanse' the filth by flooding the area. (It's Scene 49 on the cinema version of the DVD, 2 hrs 33 mins in.)

5 Invite the young people to read **Genesis 6:9 – 8:19** to each other in pairs. Ask them to think about the ways in which the episode from *The Two Towers* is the same as the Noah story. In what ways is it different? Suggest that the pairs share their thoughts with another two or three pairs.

GRACIOUS PROMISE

GENESIS 8:20 – 9:17

WHAT: *Improvisation*
WHY: *To discover more of God's grace*
WITH: *Bible, flip chart, pen*

1 Divide the young people into pairs and challenge them to prepare a short improvised drama around the following scenario: A head teacher is interviewing a new pupil for entry into their school. The pupil has been excluded from their last school for… (the young people should make up a reason, for example they burnt down the school, were a really nasty bully). The pupil should show how bad they are, with loads of attitude. The head teacher should be shocked at the pupil's behaviour and show that they don't want the pupil in their school. (They could perform these improvisations to the whole group if you have time.)

2 Read **Genesis 8:20 – 9:17** to the group and invite the young people to listen out for the promises that God makes. You could use the following questions to help:

What promise did you hear?
What does God think of people?
What does God say about the future?

3 Ask for feedback and collate the answers on the flip chart. Explain to the group that God, because he is a God of grace, has promised a great life and future even though people will continue to do wrong. This is also one of many promises that God makes to us. Now we can live life to the full and have the best life possible because of what Jesus has done for us. We can have a great relationship with God and a great future, despite the things we have done wrong.

4 In their pairs, invite the young people to improvise the school situation again. This time, whatever the pupil has done, however bad they have been, the head teacher is willing to give them a new start. What kind of future does the head teacher now talk about for the pupil?

THE PROMISE

GENESIS 12:1–9

8

WHAT: *Activity and discussion*
WHY: *To discover that God makes promises for all times*
WITH: *Copies of 'Promises, promises!' from page 15, pens, Bibles*

1 Give out copies of the 'Promises, promises!' resource page and get everyone to work through the activity.

2 Gather the group together and ask them to share what they have written down – as much as they feel comfortable to do so.

3 Read **Genesis 12:1–9** together. Draw their attention to the promises God made to Abram and explain their significance in a culture that relied upon their family line for possessions, land and food. Also explain that they may have heard of someone in the Bible called Abraham and that this is the same person but his name was changed by God later on.

4 Discuss the following questions:
• What did God promise Abram?
• Do you think God kept his promise? Why?
• Why are there some promises that we can't make?
• Why was God able to keep his promise?

5 Make the point that sometimes people let us down because they make promises, but then fail to keep them. When we make promises, we often have the best intentions, but circumstances change, often out of our control, affecting our ability to keep our promises. However, when God makes a promise, he keeps it! Nothing is out of God's control, even though sometimes it might feel like it is.

NEW NAMES

GENESIS 17

WHAT: Quiz
WHY: To trust God to keep his promises
WITH: Copies of 'Name that celebrity' from page 16, pens, Bibles, prizes

1 Hand out the 'Name that celebrity' sheet and pens, and challenge the young people to match up the showbiz and real names.

2 Once they have finished, go through the answers and give a prize to the winner(s).

3 Ask the following questions:
   • Whose real names were you most surprised by?
   • Do you think people should change their names just to help their showbiz profile?

4 Read **Genesis 17:3–5** to the group and explain that Abram's name meant 'blessed father', but God changed it to Abraham, which means 'father of many'. They may remember that God made a promise a few years back to bless Abram with countless descendants. By changing his name, God was committing to fulfill his promise. Abraham must have been a bit nervous about his new name, because he'd probably have been ridiculed if he didn't go on to have lots of descendants.

5 Finish by saying that this story is yet another example of why we can trust God to keep his promises.

ARE YOU SURE GOD?

GENESIS 22

WHAT: Reflective activity
WHY: To discover that God wants us to trust his faithfulness
WITH: Copies of the 'Quality cards' resource sheet from page 17, large sheets of paper, Bibles

1 Distribute the 'Quality cards', ideally so each young person has one card. If your group is small, you'll have to give young people more than one card. Write the following on four large sheets of paper: 'God is like this'; 'God is a little like this / God is sometimes like this'; 'God is not like this at all'; 'Not sure'. Label each corner of the room with one of the signs.

2 Get everyone to think about the 'quality' written on their card and then to go and stand in the corner they think is most appropriate. Now, find out which 'qualities' have ended up in which corner. Allow discussion about any areas of disagreement.

3 With the young people sitting in their separate corners, read, or paraphrase, **Genesis 22:1–14**. Then, ask if anyone feels their 'quality' is in the wrong corner. Provide the opportunity for the young people to move, if they want to. Get all the young people who are holding a quality of God that is seen clearly in this passage to stand up, however awkward that quality might be to understand fully.

4 Conclude by making the point that this story is set a long time ago in a culture where many people believed that the gods they worshipped required them to sacrifice children as a sign of commitment and to guarantee blessing. However, this story, along with the rest of the Bible, clearly tells us that Abraham's God, the God revealed to us in the Bible, does not want children to be sacrificed. The key to this passage is that Abraham continued to trust God in a very difficult situation and God provided. God always wants us to trust his faithfulness.

Promises, promises!

Have a look at the promises on this page and put a tick by all the promises that you can guarantee you'll keep for the next 50 years.

☐ I WILL NEVER FORGET ANY OF MY FRIENDS' BIRTHDAYS.

☐ I WILL ALWAYS BE FRIENDS WITH ...
(YOUR BEST FRIEND

☐ I WILL NEVER MISS AN EPISODE OF ...
(YOUR FAVOURITE TV PROGRAMME)

☐ I WILL NEVER GET GREY HAIR OR GO BALD.

☐ I WILL LIVE UNTIL I'M 80.

☐ I'LL NEVER GO MORE THAN 24 HOURS WITHOUT SLEEP.

☐ I WILL REMEMBER TODAY'S DATE AND THIS ACTIVITY.

☐ I WILL NEVER LOSE MY TEMPER AT MY KIDS
(WHEN/IF I HAVE SOME).

☐ I WILL ALWAYS KEEP MY PROMISES.

MAYBE YOU WOULD LIKE TO ADD SOME OF YOUR OWN...

☐ ....

☐ ....

☐ ....

☐ ....

☐ ....

The truth is, none of us can really guarantee to keep any of these promises, because we don't know what we will be doing in five years, let alone 50! Only someone who knows everything and holds the future in their hands could possibly make promises like these and be absolutely certain that they could be kept!

Name that celebrity

Many celebrities are not who they say they are! That's because they don't go by their real names but have changed their names to make them more showbiz-friendly.

So, can you match up the celebrities with their real names?

1	50 CENT		A	THOMAS MAPOTHER IV
2	TIGER WOODS		B	REGINALD KENNETH DWIGHT
3	LL COOL J		C	ELDRICK WOODS
4	MADONNA		D	QUENTIN LEO COOK
5	SNOOP DOGG		E	JAMES TODD SMITH III
6	FATBOY SLIM		F	LOUISE CICCONE
7	FERGIE		G	CURTIS JACKSON III
8	ELTON JOHN		H	CORDOZAR CALVIN BROADUS
9	DEMI MOORE		I	DEMETRIA GUYNES
10	TOM CRUISE		J	STACY FERGUSON

It would seem that names still matter when it comes to selling music and films. Names also mattered a great deal in Bible times. When God changed somebody's name, you knew that something big had been promised for that person. That's why he changed Abram's name to Abraham. Read **Genesis 17** to find out more...

ANIMAL-HATING	CHILD-HATING	SENSIBLE
CONFUSING	FAITHFUL	HALF-HEARTED
GREEDY	HOPEFUL	PROMISE-MAKER
LIAR	MURDERER	TESTING
SYMPATHETIC	OVER THE TOP	PATHETIC
PEACEFUL	POWERFUL	PROMISE-KEEPER
VIOLENT	WEIRD	WONDERFUL

Joseph

THIS POPULAR STORY IS ONE OF THE MOST WELL KNOWN IN THE BIBLE, MAINLY THROUGH ANDREW LLOYD WEBBER'S MUSICAL. SUCH A FAMILIAR STORY WILL PROVIDE YOU WITH AMPLE OPPORTUNITIES TO EXPLORE SOME OF THE THEMES BEHIND THE STORY:

- **God's in control**. If we know the story of Joseph, we read it in the knowledge that everything works out for good. But Joseph wouldn't have known that for certain as he was experiencing the events of the story. There were long periods where he must have wondered about what was happening.

- **God uses events to suit his purposes**. Joseph comments in Genesis 50:20 that God turned the evil of the brothers into good, in order to save the lives of many people.

- **God uses imperfect people**. Joseph was a boastful and foolish young man, not mature enough to use his gifts properly, but God takes him and refines him, bringing order to Egypt and reconciliation with his brothers.

These are just a few of the different aspects of the Joseph narrative you might explore. Let the young people guide you in what they discover as you read these passages together.

FOR THOSE FROM OUTSIDE A CHURCH COMMUNITY
Though young people are more likely to have heard this story, this is by no means certain. However, there is much to identify with here, even on first reading. Young people will have boastful and immature classmates (they may even be that person themselves), many will have experienced fights with siblings, they will have felt unfairly treated at one time or another, and they will also have experienced success. Make these the connecting points to the narrative, and to what God is doing.

FOR THOSE WITH A CHURCH BACKGROUND
Church young people may be over familiar with the story, so challenge them to think differently about it. Look more closely at the character of Joseph and assess how he changes through the narrative – what is God doing in his life? How is God changing him and refining his character?

WHEN THE GOING GETS TOUGH

GENESIS 37

WHAT: *Video and discussion*
WHY: *To be secure in God's faithfulness when families cause problems*
WITH: *TV and DVD player or laptop and projector, one of the following films about Joseph: for younger groups, use the Dreamworks Joseph video; for middle-of-the-age groups, use Joseph and his Amazing Technicolor Dreamcoat; and for older groups (this film has a 12 rating) use Joseph (Time Life)*

1 Beforehand, watch your chosen DVD, especially the section that covers **Genesis 37** (the coat, the dreams, Joseph's visit to his brothers in Dothan, Joseph sold into slavery in Egypt). For each session's scene, note any differences you spot between what the film says and what the Bible actually says.

2 Ask the group to think about what winds them up most about their family. How would they define the world's worst brother or sister?

3 Before you watch the film, explain that this is an adapted version of what the Bible says, and doesn't stay completely true to it. Highlight any differences you noticed between the film and the Bible version. Watch the section of the film covering **Genesis 37**.

4 Ask the group to listen for what really wound up Joseph's brothers as you (or a confident reader) read aloud **Genesis 37:1–11**. (Note: In this chapter, 'Israel' is another name for Jacob, Joseph's father.) Now ask: 'What wound Joseph's brothers up? Why do you think they got so annoyed about this? Would you want someone like Joseph as a brother? Why, or why not?' Now focus on the brothers' behaviour: 'How did Joseph's father and brothers react to him?'

5 Say that family life can be a mess sometimes, but that doesn't mean God has stopped caring or wanting good things for your family. Get the young people to close their eyes and concentrate on the words of **Psalm 100:5** as you read them aloud.

A TURN FOR THE WORST

GENESIS 39

WHAT: *Re-enactment*
WHY: *To learn to trust God when doing the right thing doesn't make life easier*
WITH: *TV and DVD player or laptop and projector, your chosen film about Joseph, CD of ambient music, CD player*

1 Find the part of your chosen Joseph film that shows the events of **Genesis 39**, from Joseph's arrival in Potiphar's house through to the success he had in prison. As before, note anywhere the film diverges from the Bible narrative and be ready to point this out to the group – the Bible is authoritative, not the film!

2 Introduce the DVD as the next part of the story of Joseph. Briefly get the young people to tell you the 'story so far'. Encourage the group to listen very carefully to the dialogue, then show your chosen clip.

3 Divide the young people into small groups of the same size as the number of key characters in your clip. So you may have Joseph, Potiphar, Potiphar's wife and a palace guard in each small group. Play the DVD with the sound down, and get the small groups to re-enact the dialogue, according to what they can see on the screen. If they're really keen, they could try to lip-sync it! They're attempting to re-tell the story with only the images to prompt them.

4 Spot which group does the best job. Get them to repeat their performance for everyone, if they're willing and if the activity hasn't taken too long so far.

5 Ask: 'What was the right thing that Joseph chose to do? What was the end result of his choosing to do the right thing?'

6 Explain that you're about to read the same story from the Bible. Ask the group to spot the name of the character who didn't actually appear in the re-enactment, and to count how many times he gets a mention. As you play some ambient music, read the whole of **Genesis 39** from the Bible. Repeat the earlier challenge to the group and get some answers. (It's God who didn't appear, but he gets a mention eight times in the Bible version.) What does this suggest about God's part in all this, even though things weren't turning out well for Joseph? So how far would you trust a God like that?

ALL IN A DAY'S WORK

GENESIS 41

13

WHAT: Quiz
WHY: To learn to be secure in God's faithfulness when there's a tough job to be done
WITH: TV and DVD player or laptop and projector, your chosen film about Joseph

1 Find the part of your chosen Joseph film that shows the events of Genesis 41, from the king's dreams through to Joseph's successful organisation of Egypt's food resources. Check the start and finish numbers on the counter for the DVD. As before, note anywhere the film diverges from the Bible narrative and be ready to point this out to the group. Also, what doesn't it show that the Bible tells us about?

2 Introduce the film clip as the next part of the story of Joseph. Briefly get the young people to tell you the 'story so far'. Show your chosen clip.

3 Mention the differences you have spotted between the film and the Bible version, as suggested in '1' above.

4 Have a quiz to check how much the group has taken in. Divide the young people into two teams – A and B. Get the teams to choose a group member to be their leader.

5 Explain the rules:

- You will fast-forward and fast-rewind the DVD between the start and finish counter numbers, but with the TV's sound turned right down (not muted) and the TV itself on standby.

- First, the leader of Team A will shout 'Stop!', and you should immediately press the stop button.

- Switch on the TV and play the film for about 30 seconds so that both teams can see (but not hear) the selected sequence.

- Note the number of characters visible on the screen the moment it starts – this will be Team A's score for this round if they are successful. Team A then has to answer two questions correctly to make that score: What exactly is happening in this sequence? What do you think God is doing here?

- Then it's Team B's turn. Start fast-forwarding and fast-rewinding again. Keep the scores as you go.

6 Before the young people lose interest, stop the game and announce the final score.

7 Ask: 'So what was the tough job Joseph was chosen to do?'; 'What was there in the film to show God's faithfulness to Joseph and to his plan?' (The answer to this one may be 'Nothing'!)

8 Ask the second question again, but this time the group will be hearing it from the Bible. Read aloud **Genesis 41:38–57** (starting with 'The king asked...'). Hear and discuss the group's suggestions.

'KNOCK, KNOCK' 'WHO'S THERE?'

GENESIS 42:1–13; 45:1–15

WHAT: Drama and film clip
WHY: To be encouraged that God's plans never fail
WITH: TV and DVD player or laptop and projector, your chosen film about Joseph

1 This follows on from last session's activity. In this session, show them when the brothers first came to see Joseph, up to when Joseph reveals to them who he is. Exactly how much you show though is up to you, and will largely depend on how the film portrays this part of Joseph's life. Make sure you watch the film before the session and decide what section you'll show.

2 Before you watch this section of the film together, tell them that they're about to see what happened when Joseph first saw his brothers after all these years. If necessary, remind the group what his brothers had done to him. Divide the young people into small groups and get them to prepare short drama sketches that show how they would have reacted towards the brothers if they had been in Joseph's shoes.

3 Get each group to perform their sketch for everyone and then show them the film. If necessary, speak to them about where the film's accounting of these events diverges from what the Bible says.

4 Discuss these three questions with the group:

• How do you think Joseph felt when he saw his brothers?
• Why do you think he didn't reveal who he was straight away?
• How do you think he felt that the dreams he'd had all those years ago had come true?

5 Explain to the group that God had given Joseph glimpses of his future. Joseph had probably held on to these during the tough times; they'd probably kept him going. God always knew what he planned for Joseph; he just needed Joseph to keep trusting him.

6 Read **Genesis 45:1–15** to the group. Make the point that it seems that Joseph loved his brothers very much and the fact that he believed God had a plan, made it easier to forgive his brothers.

7 Conclude by saying that the more secure we are in God's plan, the easier it will be to forgive and move on when people hurt us. That does not mean it will be easy; forgiveness can be extremely difficult, but it will be easier.

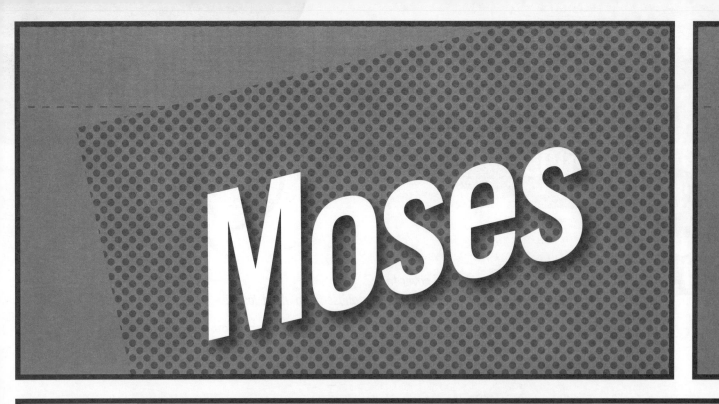

Moses

MOSES' JOURNEY FROM PRINCE TO REBEL TO LEADER OF A NATION IS ONE OF THE IMPORTANT 'ACTS' OF THE BIBLE STORY. THROUGH GOD'S POWER AND GUIDANCE, ISRAEL MOVES FROM BEING A HUGE EXTENDED FAMILY INTO BEING A NATION OF PEOPLE UNDER GOD. THE EVENTS OF THE STORY ARE REMEMBERED IN PASSOVER, ONE OF THE MOST IMPORTANT FESTIVALS IN THE CALENDAR, AND THEY ARE REFERENCED IN SUBSEQUENT BOOKS OF THE BIBLE, PARTICULARLY PSALMS, WHERE THE WRITERS REMEMBER WHAT GOD HAS DONE FOR ISRAEL.

And yet, despite seeing God in action first hand, the Israelites continually stray from his path, they whinge and complain, they turn to other gods, they doubt God's ability to provide for them and keep them safe. Their life as they move from Egypt to the Promised Land is a cycle of disobedience and repentance, with God often losing patience with his petulant nation.

And how similar are we to the Israelites? We know what God has done for us, but sometimes we conveniently forget, or it doesn't seem enough for us, or we think we can do better on our own. Consider your own life compared to the experiences of Moses and the Israelites. What does that teach you?

FOR THOSE FROM OUTSIDE A CHURCH COMMUNITY
God intervenes supernaturally many times in these passages and that might cause some discussion about whether these things are possible. Either use any such questions to talk about the all-powerful nature of God or, if your group seem too fixated by this, help them to see the purpose of God's actions, rather than focusing on the mechanics of the actions themselves. The session on the Ten Commandments might bring up questions of being 'told what to do' by God. Try to help young people see the reasons behind the Commandments.

FOR THOSE WITH A CHURCH BACKGROUND
For young people who are more familiar with the story, try to investigate ideas of these stories being part of the Israelites' psyche (it might be useful to look at passages such as Psalm 136, which explore these events). What are the equivalents for us in our lives? What has God done for us that forms part of our make up? How often do we remember those things and give thanks to God for them?

THE EGYPTIAN NIGHTMARE
Hannah MacFarlane

£5.99

PART OF THE DARK CHAPTERS SERIES THAT RETELL SOME OF THE DARKER STORIES IN THE BIBLE, THE EGYPTIAN NIGHTMARE TELLS THE STORY OF MOSES AND THE PLAGUES FROM PHARAOH'S PERSPECTIVE.

INJUSTICE

EXODUS 2:1–25

15

WHAT: *Role play/Bible study*
WHY: *To consider God's response to our cries of help*
WITH: *Bibles, or copies of the following passages: Exodus 2:1–10; 2:11–14; 2:15–25*

1 Recap the plight of the Israelites from Exodus 1 briefly: that they had moved to Egypt in the time of Joseph, but hundreds of years had passed and now the Egyptians were treating the Israelites very cruelly. The king had even passed a law saying that if an Israelite woman gave birth to a baby boy, then the boy was to be thrown into the river.

2 Split the group into three, and assign each group one of the following passages: **Exodus 2:1–10; 11–14; 15–25**. Each group should read their passage and then turn the narrative into a drama. This could be done by using a narrator to say what is happening while others act out the events, or it could all be done without a narrator, letting the characters of the play say and act what is happening. Give them five or ten minutes to rehearse and then bring everyone together.

3 Run through the whole chapter, acting out each section. Ask the members of the group who are not acting a particular section to look out for times when the people needed help.

4 Say that God doesn't always answer prayers in the way that we think he will; his help can take on many different forms. As verses 23–25 show, God knew that the Israelites – his own people – needed help.

5 Explain that the Israelites were God's people and he had made promises to them about their future. Now, because of the cruelty of the Egyptians, they needed help. God saw their troubles, was concerned and responded to their cries for help. What about the troubles people face today, such as third world debt, poverty and oppressive regimes? Do you think God cares about those? (This is a rhetorical question: obviously, he does!) So, should we be crying out to God for the problems the world faces today?

WHAT DIFFERENCE CAN I MAKE?

EXODUS 3:1 – 4:20

16

WHAT: *Thought-provoker*
WHY: *To be encouraged that each one of us plays an important part in God's world*
WITH: *Pens and paper, Bibles*

1 Ask the group what superheroes they know and what superpowers they have. Discuss briefly the differences between the characters in their 'normal' secret identity life and the superheroes they turn into (for example, Peter Parker and Spiderman).

2 Give out pens and paper, and encourage each young person to design their own superhero alter ego and the superpowers or super gadgets they would have. Chat about any reasons why they could not actually be that superhero.

3 Recap that this session's Bible events take place after the people of Israel have asked God to help them. At the time they are slaves, being harshly treated in Egypt.

4 Either get your group to read the whole passage (**Exodus 3:1 – 4:20**), or to listen while someone else reads it, or tell the story in your own words. The main points are that God heard the Israelites' call for help and chose Moses to be the instigator of his plan – but Moses didn't want to help and made as many excuses as he could.

5 Give each pair of young people a Bible and one of the following verses to identify the excuses Moses made:
3:11 *(I am not a great man.)*
4:1 *(The people won't believe me.)*
4:10 *(I am not a skilled speaker.)*
4:13 *(Couldn't you ask someone else?)*

6 Ask them to find out God's solution to Moses' complaints (**4:14–17**). Explain to the group that Moses didn't think he could be the superhero that the people of Israel needed, but with God's help, and a trusty sidekick, he was able to play a key part in God's plan of bringing his people out of slavery in Egypt.

WHY DOESN'T GOD DO SOMETHING?

EXODUS 11:1 – 12:30

WHAT: Role play and discussion
WHY: To explore the ways in which God has acted in the past
WITH: Large bed sheet, some red paint (water-based) in small pots, some cold cooked meat (lamb, if possible, make sure you know of any vegetarians in your group and offer an alternative), Bible

1   Get everyone to sit on the floor, and explain that they are the Egyptian people. Select three people to be the king, the narrator and Moses. Set the scene: the Israelites were living in Egypt, but they were slaves. They had asked God to help them as they were being treated unfairly by the Egyptians. God had responded by sending Moses to help.

2   Ask the narrator to read aloud **Exodus 11**, getting the two actors to mime the discussion as it is described. When Moses is speaking, get the actor to mime the disasters that were going to happen to the Egyptians. At this point explain that the king had become stubborn, and Moses wanted to give him a chance to change his mind. The consequences would be very serious if the king did nothing.

3   As the narrator goes on to read **Exodus 12**, the king and Moses come out of character and hand around the meat on a plate. (Be aware of hygiene and allergy issues as well as any vegetarians.)

4   Let the young people eat it. The two actors who distributed the meat can then put small dabs of red paint on the forehead of some of the young people.

5   When the narrator gets to **12:29**, the two actors should pass the sheet over the group on the floor. Explain that those with red paint on their forehead can stay sitting up, while those without paint should lie down as if they are dead. Then read verse **30**.

6   Ask those who are dead to sit up again! Then ask those who are alive to separate from them. Remind the group of verses **24–28** again. Encourage the group to listen carefully to what you are reading. Explain that the Jews still celebrate this event as a reminder of what God did to save his people.

7   Conclude by saying that neither circumstances nor people ever defeat God. Here we have seen God intervening in a very dramatic way for his people to be released from captivity. God uses people to make his plans happen. So how can he use us in the global problems that are happening around the world? Does God want us to help the creation he loves?

FREEDOM

EXODUS
14:1–31

WHAT: *Dramatic interpretation of Bible passage*
WHY: *To thank God that he can lead, and has led, the oppressed to freedom*
WITH: *Copies of 'Who do you trust?' questionnaire from page 28, Bibles*

1   Individually, let the group members read and complete the 'Who do you trust?' questionnaire.

2   In pairs, encourage the young people to discuss their reactions to the questions. Explain that God isn't in any of the options offered. Get the pairs to look at the questionnaire again and ask themselves if they would trust God in any of the situations. Why, or why not?

3   Bring the group together again. Divide them into small groups of about six to eight. In each group, one person represents Moses, one is the King of Egypt, a couple are the Israelites and a couple are the Egyptian soldiers. If you don't have enough people for all the parts, get each person in the group to change from one character to another as they are mentioned in the story.

4   Either you, or a confident reader from the group, should read Exodus 14 slowly and dramatically. While it is being read, the groups act out the various parts.

5   Allow for breaks in the reading, to ask questions and allow a short time of discussion:

   • After **Exodus 14:4**, say to Moses: 'You have led the Israelites to freedom, but now God is calling you to turn back towards the Egyptians, your enemy. Why is God asking you to do this?'

   • After **Exodus 14:9**, ask the King of Egypt: 'How do you feel about these Israelites whom you relied on as your slaves and who now demand freedom?'

   • After **Exodus 14:12**, ask the Israelites: 'Why might you be thinking life in Egypt is better? Is freedom worth a fight? Why, or why not?'

   • After **Exodus 14:20**, ask the Egyptian soldiers: 'Why do you think the cloud has moved?'

   • After **Exodus 14:28**, ask the Israelites: 'How do you feel about what has just happened?'

   • After **Exodus 14:31**, ask all the young people to drop their characters and be themselves and then ask: 'If you had just walked through a sea through which God had cleared a path, what would you say about him?'

6   Explain that God cares about the oppressed and longs for their freedom. The Israelites cried out for help but then had to trust that God would help save them from the Egyptians.

THE TOP TEN DOS AND DON'TS

EXODUS 20:1–17

WHAT: *Sorting*
WHY: *To examine how to do God's will*
WITH: *Paper, pens, copies of 'Commandment cards' from page 29, flip chart or large sheet of paper, Bibles*

1 Divide the group into small teams of between two and five players. Cut out enough copies of the 'Commandment cards' to give each team a set, and ask them to spread them out where they can all see them. Say you're looking for the top five commandments.

2 Give the teams time to read them; then give them one minute to sort the commandments for each category below. On a flip chart sheet, keep a score for each commandment, giving each one a point every time it is featured in a top five. Don't worry if the ridiculous ones score high – this is to be expected:

• The top five commandments you ought to live by to make the world a better place.

• The top five commandments other people should live by to make the world a better place.

• The top five commandments everyone in the world throughout history ought to live by to make the world a better place.

The top five commandments that show us the best way to live.

3 Declare which commandments are the top five overall. If these points haven't arisen already, point out that some people think God gave his Ten Commandments to make life miserable and restricted. Explain, however, that God was really trying to show his people the best way to live – just like following the maker's instructions is the best way to use a new gadget so you don't break it and to get to know about all its cool features. God shows us how to love him and how to love other people. God also chose advice that would be good for all people everywhere throughout all history.

4 Still in their small groups and using paper and pens, challenge the young people to list the Ten Commandments that God gave to Moses. Give the groups a couple of minutes. Remind them that God wants to show us the best way to live (how to love God and love other people) – not the easiest way.

5 Check them against **Exodus 20:1–17** by reading it to the group.

BE BIG

JOSHUA 1

20

WHAT: *Drama*
WHY: *To grow more confident in God*
WITH: *The 'Joshua' script below; each verse of Joshua 1:2–9 printed out on a separate card and numbered*

1 Get a volunteer to sit on a chair in front of the others and introduce him as Joshua, using the script below.

2 Divide the group in half. Tell one team that they must try to persuade Joshua to wimp out. The other team must persuade Joshua to cross the raging river and take hold of the Promised Land. Give each of them one minute to prepare and note down a few ideas.

3 In turn, each team now has one minute to try and convince Joshua they have the best idea. At the end of the time, the young person playing Joshua should choose which advice to follow. Say that this was a decision that the real Joshua had to face. But he didn't have mixed advice – God gave him a pep talk that would see him through the tough times ahead.

4 Give different young people the verses on numbered cards and ask them to read them out. Say that this was God's pep talk to Joshua. Ask the young people to choose which piece of encouragement they think Joshua would find most useful. Say that when we face challenging times – even when the people we rely on let us down or disappear – we can have courage and be confident in God, just as Joshua did.

5 Ask the group to think of a difficult change that they're facing at the moment, or will be facing soon – a new class at school, a new activity, a house move or a change in their family or group of close friends. Encourage them to picture that situation and, in their minds, just to give it to God, asking God to be with them as he was with Joshua.

JOSHUA SCRIPT

JOSHUA. HIS DAD'S CALLED NUN, BUT HE CAN'T HELP THAT, AND UP TO NOW HE HAS BEEN MOSES' RIGHT-HAND MAN – LIKE HELPING OUT WHEN GOD GAVE MOSES THE TEN COMMANDMENTS. BUT NOW MOSES IS DEAD AND JOSHUA IS THE NEW LEADER. BOTH JOSHUA AND GOD'S PEOPLE HAVE A CHOICE TO MAKE. WILL THEY GO FORWARD OR BACKWARDS?

JUST IN FRONT OF JOSHUA IS THE RAGING RIVER JORDAN. ON THE OTHER SIDE OF THE RIVER IS THE LAND THAT GOD HAS PROMISED WILL BE THEIRS – HOME AT LAST AFTER ALL THAT WANDERING ROUND THE DESERT! BUT MOSES IS DEAD, SO PERHAPS JOSHUA DOESN'T FEEL TOO CONFIDENT ABOUT CROSSING THE RAGING RIVER AND TAKING HOLD OF THE LAND. THE PROMISED LAND SHOULD BE THEIRS, BUT THE PEOPLE ALREADY LIVING THERE DON'T EXACTLY KNOW IT YET AND THERE'LL BE LOTS OF FIGHTING AND UPHEAVAL AHEAD. IT'S TOUGH WITHOUT MOSES LEADING THE WAY.

SO HERE'S THE CHOICE: JOSHUA COULD WIMP OUT AND TELL THE ISRAELITES TO FIND ANOTHER LEADER, OR LEAD THEM BACK INTO THE DESERT THE WAY THEY CAME, OR HE COULD LEAD THEM ON INTO THE PROMISED LAND.

Who do you trust?

1

YOU ARE TRYING ON A NEW PAIR OF JEANS. WHO WOULD YOU TRUST TO TELL YOU WHAT THEY LOOKED LIKE?

- Your boyfriend/girlfriend
- Your gran
- No one – I would decide myself

2

YOU ARE BEING PICKED ON AT SCHOOL; A GROUP OF OLDER KIDS ARE FOLLOWING YOU AROUND AND DEMANDING YOUR DINNER MONEY. WHO WOULD YOU TRUST TO SORT OUT THE SITUATION?

- The biggest, strongest lad you know
- A teacher
- One of your parents

3

YOU ARE ON A SCHOOL TRIP IN FRANCE WHEN YOU GET SEPARATED FROM THE GROUP. YOU REALISE YOU ARE LOST. WHO WOULD YOU TRUST TO HELP YOU OUT?

- A young person on the train
- A police officer
- The old man offering you a lift back to your hotel

4

ONE OF YOUR FRIENDS THINKS SHE IS PREGNANT. WHO WOULD YOU TRUST TO HELP HER?

- The first aid person at school
- Your church minister
- A doctor

5

YOU REALLY FANCY SOMEONE AT SCHOOL BUT YOU'RE NOT SURE WHAT TO DO NEXT. WHO WOULD YOU TRUST TO GIVE YOU ADVICE?

- Your star sign chart
- Your best friend
- Your pet dog, Scampy

COMMANDMENT CARDS

1 YOU MUST NOT HAVE ANY OTHER GODS.

2 YOU MUST WASH YOUR HANDS BEFORE EATING.

3 YOU MUST NOT SQUEEZE YOUR PIMPLES OR ANYONE ELSE'S.

4 YOU MUST NOT MAKE IDOLS OR WORSHIP THEM.

5 YOU MUST NOT USE THE NAME OF THE LORD YOUR GOD THOUGHTLESSLY.

6 YOU MUST BE KIND TO ANIMALS, ESPECIALLY YOUR OX AND DONKEY.

7 YOU MUST NOT PLAY BALL GAMES ON THE GRASS.

8 REMEMBER TO KEEP THE SABBATH DAY HOLY.

9 HONOUR YOUR FATHER AND MOTHER.

10 BE NICE TO YOUR BROTHERS AND SISTERS.

11 YOU MUST NOT DO ANYTHING ENJOYABLE, AS IT IS PROBABLY SINFUL.

12 YOU MUST NOT MURDER ANYONE.

13 YOU MUST NOT BE GUILTY OF ADULTERY.

14 YOU MUST NOT WATCH CERT 18 FILMS WHEN YOU ARE ONLY 13.

15 YOU MUST NOT OFFEND YOUR NEIGHBOUR.

16 YOU MUST NOT STEAL.

17 YOU MUST NOT TELL LIES ABOUT YOUR NEIGHBOUR.

18 YOU MUST EAT FIVE PORTIONS OF FRUIT AND VEGETABLES EVERY DAY.

19 YOU MUST NOT WANT TO TAKE YOUR NEIGHBOUR'S PROPERTY.

20 YOU MUST PUT DOWN THE TOILET LID BEFORE LEAVING THE BATHROOM.

David

DAVID IS ONE OF THE HEROES OF THE BIBLE, ONE OF JESUS' ANCESTORS AND FREQUENTLY REFERENCED IN THE NEW TESTAMENT. HE IS AN IMPORTANT CHARACTER TO EXPLORE IF WE'RE GOING TO HELP YOUNG PEOPLE GET AN UNDERSTANDING OF THE STORY OF THE BIBLE.

However, like so many other Bible 'heroes', David is sometimes anything but heroic. Unregarded by his father at the start of the narrative, David goes on to be the greatest king Israel has ever had (not counting Jesus of course...), but he still got things wrong, still worked towards what he wanted at times, still misunderstood what God was doing.

The story of David and Goliath is likely to be the one that most young people have heard of (though it still may be relatively unknown!), yet it is David and Bathsheba which may make the most impact. Many young people don't expect this kind of story to appear in the Bible ('It's like EastEnders in the Bible!'), so it may be a chance to explore ideas of lust, lies, covering up and facing the consequences – all relevant topics in many young people's lives.

FOR THOSE FROM OUTSIDE A CHURCH COMMUNITY

David is a great personality for those outside a church community to start with – he is a man who loves God and yet he still gets it wrong. Through the four stories in this section, important aspects of God's character will come forward – a God who knows our potential rather than only seeing our exterior, a God who protects, a God who keeps his promises, a God who is just and forgiving.

FOR THOSE WITH A CHURCH BACKGROUND

Many young people from a church background will think they know David. But a re-examining of the familiar stories, together with opening up some of the lesser-known ones, will help young people get a better picture of David, rather than just the giant-slayer! Psalm 136 provides young people with the chance to look back at their lives so far and remember what God has done for them. But here, the writer thanks God for some unusual things! Use these as stimuli for a discussion on things we might need to thank God for. Would David thank God for the start of his relationship with Bathsheba?

ABOUT A BOY

1 SAMUEL 16:1–13

21

WHAT: *Game*

WHY: *To see how God provides for his people*

WITH: *Basic grocery provisions (including some olive oil), a Bible, a picture of the Prime Minister, a bottle of water, a small box labelled 'medicine', an image of a house and a text book all on a tray, flip chart (optional)*

1 Make the point that God provides for his people. But what are people's needs? Brainstorm the difference between what we want and what we need. (Make two lists on a flip chart if necessary.)

2 Show the group the items on the tray and say that these provide the basic necessities for life – food, water, shelter, health, education, leadership, God. Explain that in one minute's time you will take one of the items away. The young people will have to work out which one you have removed. Briefly hide the tray from view and remove an item. Show the tray again and get everyone to guess which item was removed.

3 Repeat the exercise until only one item, the picture of the Prime Minister, is left. (Gradually decrease the viewing time for each round, down to five seconds for the last two objects.) Discuss whether this would be everyone's choice, if they could only choose one of the essential items.

4 Read or paraphrase the story of David's election to the position of leader and king in **1 Samuel 16:1–13**. You could act it out by having seven volunteers stand in line (with an eighth – 'David' – hiding behind them) and rejecting them one by one until only 'David' is left.

5 Demonstrate what anointing is by marking the forehead of the eighth volunteer with the olive oil.

6 Discuss together why the provision of a leader is so important to some people:

- What would life be like with no leaders?
- Would it work at all or would some people assume or be given leadership responsibility without any official title?

Ask the young people:
- Does your friendship group have a natural leader or organiser?
- How did that come about?
- Do you think God was involved in the process?

7 Finally, take a vote:
- Is leadership a natural talent (something that you're born with), a developed skill (people can be trained), or both?
- Which way is the most common in your experience?
- Which way do they think God would use the most? Pray briefly that God will continue to provide everyone with what they need.

HUNKY GORY

1 SAMUEL
17:1 – 18:5

Open Doors Step 3

22

WHAT: *Story with illustration and discussion*
WHY: *To develop our potential as God's people*
WITH: *'David and Goliath' story script from page 34, measuring tape*

1 This session's Bible passage (**1 Samuel 17:1 – 18:5**) is a captivating story. Read aloud the 'David and Goliath' story script.

2 Use volunteers, and if necessary a measuring tape, to demonstrate the comparative heights of the two men (Goliath was more than nine feet tall). For safety's sake, get them to do this lying on the floor.

3 Discuss what enabled David to reach his full potential as a giant-killer. In smaller groups, if necessary, encourage everyone to discuss these questions:
• In what aspects of your life do you feel you have potential but are unable to achieve it? What's stopping you?
• What practical steps could be taken to overcome these obstacles?
• What is the potential of God's people? What could they become and do? What's stopping them?
• What practical steps could be taken to overcome these obstacles?

4 End with this quote. Evangelist J John says David could have had one of two possible attitudes when he faced the giant Goliath: 'He's so big; I'd better run away' or 'He's so big; how can I miss?'

THINKING BIG

2 SAMUEL 7

Open Doors step 5

23

WHAT: *Newsflash!*
WHY: *To hear how elated David was by God's plans for, and promises to, his family*
WITH: *Pens and paper, Bibles, small rewards (optional)*

1 Read the story from **2 Samuel 7** in advance and then paraphrase or retell the story to the group as creatively as possible (you could use different voices for the characters, or act out the reading with a co-leader).

2 Invite the young people to reflect on what they thought about the story by discussing it with them and answering any questions. You could make this fun by explaining before telling the story that they will be quizzed on it afterwards. Then ask questions with no 'right' answers (such as 'What was your favourite bit?') and offer a small reward (such as a sweet) to each person who gives an answer.

3 Give out pens and paper, and encourage the young people to summarise the story as a news article, using their own words. They might like to work in pairs or small groups. Alternatively, they could draw a comic strip.

4 Share their summaries, and finish by asking how David felt at the end of the story. Why did he feel like this? (Because of God's promise.) What did he do to show how he felt? (He praised God.)

GOING WRONG

2 SAMUEL 11:1 – 12:15

Open Doors Step 4

24

WHAT: *Magazine activity*
WHY: *To hear that God did not give up on David, even when he broke God's rules*
WITH: *'If God gave up on us' flow chart from page 35, Bibles*

1. Read **2 Samuel 11:1 – 12:15** together as a group.

2. Ask the young people for their initial reactions to the passage. What parts stick out for them? Are they surprised at all? Why?

3. Explain that although David was punished and suffered the consequences for his actions, God still allowed him to be king. David broke nearly all of God's rules (the Ten Commandments) in one go, but God did not give up on David; he forgave him and continued to be with him.

4. Ask the group these two rhetorical questions to think about:
   • If you, or a friend, did something really terrible, like David did, do you think God would forgive you/them?
   • Do you think God would ever give up on someone? Do you think he already has?

5. Give out copies of the 'If God gave up on us' flow chart and get everyone to read through it individually.

6. Bring everyone back together and invite feedback.

7. Close in prayer for the group.

EVERLASTING LOVE

PSALM 136

Open Doors Step 2

25

WHAT: *Antiphonal reading*
WHY: *To give thanks to God for all that he has done*
WITH: *The words of Psalm 136 displayed on a screen or copied onto sheets of paper*

1. Give out copies of **Psalm 136** or display the words on a screen. Divide the young people into two groups. One group should read the first half of each verse, the other the second half.

2. After you have read the psalm, ask the first group to recall as many things to give thanks for as they can, without looking.

3. Ask the second group why they think every verse has the refrain about thankfulness. (To get the point across, or because Israel kept forgetting, or because people find it hard to remember love when things are hard.)

4. Encourage the young people to think about what they might have to be thankful about. Challenge them to think of ways in which they can be thankful through the tough times as well as when they are happy.

David and Goliath

It was a standoff – the Israelite army on one hill, the Philistines on the other. They faced each other. They taunted each other. Neither side wanted to attack because in warfare defending higher ground gives you an advantage. So across the valley they traded insults.
'You cowards.'
'You wimps.'
'Come and have a go if you think you're hard enough.'
'We'll fold you in half.'

The Philistines had a big bloke. Seriously big and then bigger still. His armour alone was heavy enough to kill an ordinary Israelite soldier. He was so big he couldn't lift a shield big enough to protect himself as well as all his weapons, so a bloke went in front of him carrying it. Tough job.

The big bloke suggested, tauntingly of course, that they forget the 'army versus army' thing and do the 'one man versus one man' thing. Winner takes all. This would have saved a lot of bloodshed, but had one small drawback. Whoever stepped forward from the Israelite army was very likely to get folded in half and half again and end up becoming fertiliser for Philistine crops. So, no great rush to volunteer then.

The Israelite king even offered incentives such as tax breaks, treasure and one of his daughters, but still no one took their chance. Maybe his daughters weren't that pretty. Who knows?

For forty days the big Philistine issued his challenge. Once in the morning and once in the evening without a day off, so you have to admire his stamina. His name was Goliath, which isn't Hebrew for 'big, ugly, taunty bloke'. David had some brothers in the Israelite army and, since he had heard they weren't actually fighting at the time but only involved in a slanging match, he went to see if his brothers were OK. He took them cheese as a gift, so let's hope it wasn't a long journey.

When he got there he happened to hear the big, ugly, taunty bloke do his big, ugly, taunty thing. David made a few enquiries about why Goliath hadn't had his head cut off yet and his brothers got a bit naffed off at this, suggesting that leaving his sheep by themselves wasn't the smartest thing David had ever done, but thanks for the cheese. They thought he'd come to watch the battle, which was a big spectator sport in those days as it took place in a small area rather than everywhere, and you could usually find a safe place to watch.

So David offered to show them he was serious by going and fighting Goliath. Everyone told him he would be folded in like about nine or something because they weren't that good at maths, and David said, 'Whatever' but he was used to killing lions and bears and, anyway, God had told him to do it – which sounds a bit intimidating. They said 'OK' whilst sniggering into their hands a bit and checking their maths.

So Saul, the king, had David dressed in armour and when David got up nothing happened because it was a bit heavier than cheese.

David took the armour off, checked his arms and legs still worked, and went to get some stones for his sling. He hadn't told anyone he was going to win by superior weapons technology, mainly because they didn't understand the words 'superior', 'weapons' or 'technology'.

David moved towards Goliath who set out, quite clearly, his new fertiliser recipe that involved quite a lot of David. David liked this idea and shouted his own fertiliser recipe back. It was an improved recipe because it had better ingredients. OK. More ingredients.

Goliath ran at David who ran at David who ran at Goliath who… well, you get the picture. Then Goliath stopped because a stone in the forehead tends to do that to a man. He had a surprised look on his face and a not-working look on the rest of him. David cut Goliath's head off with his own sword since he didn't seem to be needing it any more. The rest of the Philistines ran away to become part of the much-improved fertiliser recipe at Gath, which isn't Philistine for 'grow-bag'.

David kept Goliath's head for himself, which was a bit morbid.

And King Saul said to David, 'Whose son are you?' And David said, 'Jesse's' which was the truth although not the sort of thing it was wise to say to a king without explanation.

And then it all got dreadfully complicated. David became popular, the king's son Jonathan became his best mate and gave him pressies, and Saul gave him promotion. But Saul also began to get the teeniest bit jealous.

If God gave up on us

God will never give up on us. God's love, acceptance and forgiveness are some of life's greatest constants. But because they are always there, sometimes they can be taken for granted. Sometimes to appreciate the things we have, it helps to think about what life would be like if we didn't have them.

Below is a flow chart to show the contrast in our lives if God gave up on us.

WE DO SOMETHING REALLY BAD
(SIN AGAINST GOD BY BREAKING HIS RULES)

GOD GIVES UP ON US	GOD DOES NOT GIVE UP ON US
God lets us carry on as we are – We carry on unaware of our mistakes or why we feel guilty	**God shows us where we have gone wrong –** We have the chance to accept and understand our mistakes
God ignores us – Any prayers we might make are ignored	**God allows us to approach him –** We can pray to God for forgiveness
God does not forgive us – We are not forgiven	**God forgives us –** We are forgiven
God does not take away our sin – We are left with our feelings of guilt and sadness	**God takes away our sin –** We are free from guilt and sadness
God chooses to remember our sin – We can never escape what we did	**God chooses to forget our sin –** We can start afresh
God does not comfort us – We are left feeling worthless and a failure	**God comforts us –** He gives hope and tell us he has a plan for us
God rejects us as his children – We do not know his love	**God reaffirms us as his child –** We can know his unconditional love
God refuses us any more guidance – We are not allowed to read the Bible any more	**God guides us and helps us –** We can read the Bible and learn to be wise
God will never speak to us again – We can't feel God's Spirit any more	**God continues to speak to us –** He speaks to us through his Spirit
God wipes us from the face of the planet – We are wiped out from the earth	**God reaffirms his commitment to humankind –** We will never be wiped from the earth
God condemns us for all eternity – We cannot enter heaven to be with God	**God offers us salvation for all eternity –** We can enter heaven and be with God
GOD HAS COMPLETELY GIVEN UP ON US	GOD WILL NEVER GIVE UP ON US

Exile

THE EXILE IS AN IMPORTANT PART OF THE LARGER STORY OF THE BIBLE, BUT IS ONE THAT IS NOT WIDELY KNOWN OR EXPLORED BY YOUNG PEOPLE. HOWEVER, THE NARRATIVES CONCERNING THIS TIME OF ISRAEL'S HISTORY HAVE A GREAT DEAL TO SAY ABOUT GOD AND OUR RELATIONSHIP WITH HIM.

Following centuries of the people of Israel and Judah turning against God, God allowed the large empires to the east to invade and scatter God's people. In 722 BC, Israel, the northern kingdom, was conquered by the Assyrian Empire and parts of the population were deported to Assyria. In 586 BC, Judah was finally laid waste by the Babylonian Empire, the Temple was destroyed and much of the population deported to Babylon.

The stories of Jeremiah and Daniel talk of God being faithful, despite the suffering the people are going through. The passage from Isaiah recalls the promises that God has already made – that he will send a Messiah to save the people. For a people in deep despair, maybe hundreds of miles from their homeland, remembering this is a deep comfort.

FOR THOSE FROM OUTSIDE A CHURCH COMMUNITY

The stories from Daniel present a picture that is not often seen in the media or the news – someone standing up for what they believe in, no matter what difficulties or dangers they face. Daniel's stance may well be surprising to some, who are more used to seeing people fall and fail in soaps and other media. Here is a man who will not back down, not compromise, not turn his back on God. Spend some time exploring what this might mean in terms of following God – what does he call us to? What do young people make of Daniel's uncompromising stand?

FOR THOSE WITH A CHURCH BACKGROUND

The Daniel stories may well be known to those with a church background. However, challenge them to look at the narratives with new eyes – what do they make of Daniel's actions? The stories in Jeremiah may be less familiar to them, but are no less challenging. Let young people really get to grips with what God is saying here – are they ready to be disciplined and changed by God, so that they can walk more closely with him?

WHATEVER

26

JEREMIAH
18:1–12

WHAT: *Drama and discussion*
WHY: *To understand that some people will not accept God*
WITH: *Copies of the 'Jerry Zinger Show' script from page 41*

1. Give out copies of the 'Jerry Zinger Show' script. Choose someone to play each character.

2. Read **Jeremiah 18:1–12** so that everyone is familiar with the story. Then read through the sketch.

3. Get the young people to discuss the sketch. Do they want to add in a dialogue of their own? Talk about any changes they want to make, without removing the central story.

4. Encourage the young people to act out the sketch together. Encourage your group to improvise a stage set and get everyone who is not in the sketch to be the audience.

5. When you have finished, chat together about why the people of Judah didn't want to listen to God. Talk about the chance that God was giving them. You may want to ask:

   • Which is easier to do: what you want or what someone else wants?
   • What difference do you think the illustration of the potter made to the people of Judah?
   • What chance was God giving them?

BATTLE RE-ENACTMENT PICTURES

HOPE SPRINGS ETERNAL

JEREMIAH
31:1–6; 32:1–15

*Open Doors
step 9*

WHAT: *Battle re-enactment*
WHY: *To know that we can live with hope because of God's knowledge and power*
WITH: *A sheet of flip chart paper with the word 'Jerusalem' written at the top, 'Battle re-enactment' pictures copied from page 37 and cut out in advance*

1 Put the flip chart paper on the floor and explain that this sheet is now like a map of Jerusalem. Explain that we are going to lay out on the map the situation that Jeremiah was facing in today's passage, to help us understand what things were like for him.

2 Hand out the 'Battle re-enactment' pictures so that everyone has at least one. Explain that you are now going to read out a summary of today's Bible passage and that each person should place (and remove) their picture on the paper at the point in the story where it is mentioned.

3 Read out the summary below. You may want to stop halfway through the story and ask how they would have felt if they had been stuck in prison in the middle of Jerusalem at the time the soldiers were surrounding it. Then continue to read out the Bible summary.

So, this is the scene: Jez is having a seriously bad day. There he is sat in the middle of Jerusalem. *(Put the Jeremiah picture in the middle of the paper.)* There are houses all around him *(Put the pictures of houses scattered around where Jeremiah is.)* when the next thing he knows the king throws him in the prison *(Put the prison picture in the middle of the piece of paper and Jeremiah on top of it.)* in the middle of Jerusalem. His crime? Telling people what God is saying. This is not a good day.

Just when you think things couldn't get any worse, our mate Jez remembers that being in prison isn't his only problem. The city is surrounded by Babylonian soldiers. *(Put the pictures of soldiers on paper so they surround all the houses in Jerusalem.)* They stretch all the way around the city – and any moment they are going to invade. There is no way for anyone to get out – the city and everyone in it seem doomed.

Then, in the middle of all this God tells Jez to do something that seems really… well… er… odd. God tells Jez to buy a field in Jerusalem. *(Place the picture of a flower in the Jerusalem area – inside the area surrounded by soldiers.)* So that's exactly what he does. While he's in prison in a city that is surrounded by an army about to rip it to shreds, Jez buys a field in the city.

This is the reason why – Jez says, 'God has told me, "Things are going to be tough. This city is going to get invaded by the army *(Move the soldiers inward on the paper.)* and loads of houses will be destroyed. *(Rip up the houses.)* But I have told Jez to buy a field as a way of showing you that even though many houses will be destroyed and even though loads of people will be killed, this is still a place worth investing in. There is hope for this city. *(Remove soldiers and prison so only Jeremiah and flower remain.)* One day people will want to buy the land here again. Though times are tough now, things will get better."'

4 When you have finished, ask the young people why they think Jeremiah bought a field in the middle of a siege – what was this a sign of? Get two confident readers to read **Jeremiah 32:1–15** and **Jeremiah 31:1–6**.

5 Make the point that, if we are living to please God then God promises that, although things may be hard and seem hopeless at times, ultimately he will bring good things to those who trust him (**Revelation 21:3–5**).

JUST SAY 'NO'

DANIEL 1

28

WHAT: *Bible study and quiz*
WHY: *To explore where to draw the line in our actions in order to remain faithful to God*
WITH: *Copies of 'Enough evidence?' questionnaire from page 42, Bibles*

1 Read **Daniel 1** to the young people. Explain that Daniel had been taken prisoner and was living in a foreign country. Explain that Daniel wouldn't eat the food the king was providing because it was food offered to other gods. As a believer in God, Daniel did not want to offend God by doing this.

2 Ask the group these questions:
  • What was the deal that Daniel made with the king's servant **(vs 11–13)**?
  • What was the outcome after ten days **(v 15)**?

3 Make the point that God honoured Daniel and his friends (by making them healthier than everyone else and more successful than others) for choosing to not do something that would upset him.

4 Give out copies of the 'Enough evidence?' questionnaire. Ask the young people to complete it in pairs or threes. After a few minutes, get everyone back together to discuss their answers.

STICK TO THE TRUTH

DANIEL 6

29

WHAT: *Drawing*
WHY: *To remain loyal to God, even when living God's way could get us into trouble*
WITH: *Script from page 40, long sheets of paper (wallpaper is ideal), felt-tip pens, a tape measure, some bags of sugar or weights*

1 Read out the script from page 40 (this is an overview of **Daniel 6**).

2 Explain that you are going to imagine how Daniel must have felt when he faced the lions. To help, you're going to mark out the rough size and weight of the lions he may have faced. If you have a larger group (and room!) you may like to split into smaller groups and each mark out a lion size.

3 Get each group to create a sheet of paper 260 cm long and 120 cm high. They may need to stick a few lengths of wallpaper together. Suggest that they lay it out on the floor. Challenge them to draw a lion to these dimensions:

head and body length: 240 cm
tail length: 70 cm (this will need to curl around to fit on the paper!)
height: 110 cm

4 Get each group to compare the size of their lions with a young person.

5 Give each group a bag of sugar (or a weight) and tell them how many bags of sugar (or weights) the lion would weigh. (They weigh about 225 kg.) Decide as a group whether a human or a lion would have the best chance of survival if they were locked in a room together.

6 Ask the group to think back to the article you read out earlier. Ask these questions:

  • If you were in Daniel's situation, how might you have felt at these times:
    before you prayed?
    when you were brought to the king?
    when you were thrown in with the lions?
  • If you were in Daniel's situation, what would you have done?
  • Are there times when doing the right thing has meant that you've taken a risk?
  • If God rescued Daniel from the lions, do you think that God can help you in these situations?

PARTY TIME!

ISAIAH 9:2–7;
LUKE 1:26–33

30

WHAT: *Drawing*
WHY: *To celebrate that God has shown us his glory by giving us his Son*
WITH: *Large copies of the two Bible passages, highlighter pens, flip chart or large sheet of paper, marker pens*

1 Spend some time chatting about the different things the young people celebrate. With that air of celebration in mind, read **Isaiah 9:2–7** together. Give out copies of the Bible passage and highlighter pens and ask the young people to highlight all the parts of the passage that they think are worth celebrating.

2 When everyone has finished, talk about what the young people have highlighted. Write anything that the whole group agrees about on a flip chart or large sheet of paper. Invite any comments about those things.

3 In a different colour, write the things that only a few people thought were worth celebrating. Ask people why they thought some things were worth celebrating and ask others why they didn't agree. Encourage some healthy discussion here, but if your group is reluctant to talk, don't try to force it.

4 Now read **Luke 1:26–33** in the same way, highlighting the things that are worth celebrating. This time, ask the group to look out for similarities between the two passages and underline them. When everyone is done, obtain feedback and look at the similarities together. Comment that the events prophesied by Isaiah came about here, with Mary and Jesus. What does that tell the group about God?

DANIEL 6 OVERVIEW

Talk about a bunch of back-stabbers. I never asked to be serving the king in this country. I never asked to be promoted above them all. In case they forget, I was taken by force and brought to this land. All I have done is try to serve God and keep loyal to him. So what do I get for it – those people, who are supposed to be under me, going off to the king and getting him to make a new law so that no one is allowed to pray to anyone except the king! And the punishment for breaking the law? Death. Not a quick or easy death either – being thrown to the lions is what they decided on.

Well, what would you do? Do you stay true to God, keep praying and risk being put to death, or do you ease off the praying for a bit? Keep your head low? Well, I decided to stay loyal to God – even if it might cost me my life.

Sure enough, before you know it, I am dragged in front of the king and thrown into the lions' den. Loads of them in there. A big stone is rolled over the front of the cave. There's nowhere to go.

I can't tell you how it happened, but somehow I survived. None of the lions even came near me. I knew God had protected me. The next day the king was so relieved to see me alive and without a scratch on me. He had never wanted me thrown to the lions and he didn't take long to make amends. First thing he did was to get those back-stabbers who had set me up and threw them to the lions instead. I won't go into detail, but let's say, the lions didn't pass up the chance of a good meal. Then the king issued another decree – but this one says that everyone in the land should give total respect to God. Now that's what I call a result!

Jerry Zinger Show

THE CHARACTERS

JERRY ZINGER: IRREPRESSIBLE TALK SHOW HOST
JEREMIAH: SLIGHTLY TATTERED PROPHET OF GOD
THE PEOPLE OF JUDAH: THE STUBBORN PEOPLE OF GOD
MR POTTER: THE SIMPLE POTTER AT WHOSE HOUSE JEREMIAH FIRST HAD HIS MESSAGE FROM GOD

JERRY: Good evening and welcome to the Jerry Zinger show! On the show tonight: the crazy prophet of doom who is driving Judah mad, Jeremiah! *(Jeremiah enters and takes a seat.)* So, Jeremiah, just what is it you have to say that is driving God's people so crazy? Why are you so deeply unpopular?

JEREMIAH: Well, Jerry, I guess it's because I won't tell them what they want to hear. I tell them what God wants me to say.

JERRY: And just what is it that God wants you to say, Jeremiah? Or can I call you Jerry?

JEREMIAH: Er, yes, I suppose you can. *(Clears his throat.)* This is the word of the Lord. *(Reads* **Jeremiah 18:6–12**. *Silence for a moment after he finishes reading. Jerry looks puzzled.)*

JERRY: Well, that's certainly fascinating. What does it all mean? Here to give us the other side of the story, please give a big Jerry Zinger welcome to... The People of Judah! *(The People of Judah enter in a group and take their seats.)* So, Judah, what have you got to say to Jeremiah?

JUDAH: He's just an old misery. He's always coming up with prophecies about our destruction. And look, we are still here! If God is so mad with us, why doesn't he just smite us right here and now? Eh? Eh?

JEREMIAH: *(Trying to be patient.)* Because for some reason, far beyond my understanding, he wants to give you the chance to change your ways. He wants you to submit willingly to him. He wants you to be obedient so that he can bless you.

JUDAH: You just want to try and control us. You don't want us to be ourselves. You want everyone to be miserable, like you.

JERRY: OK, people, let's keep calm now. There's just one other person who might be able to help us understand this situation. Please welcome, Mr Potter! *(Mr Potter wanders in, looking a bit confused.)* Hello Mr Potter. I understand that it was at your house that Jeremiah received this message from God.

MR POTTER: Ar, I believe he did.

JERRY: So, Mr Potter, what we're all dying to know is, what does he look like?

MR POTTER: Who? Jeremiah?

JERRY: No, not Jeremiah! The big G. GOD!

MR POTTER: I don't rightly know. I didn't see 'im or nuffin.

JERRY: You didn't see him.

MR POTTER: No...

JERRY: So, this message, how did it arrive?

MR POTTER: Don't rightly know. Thar I was, working on me pots, and suddenly Jeremiah starts talkin' about how we's all a bit like clay in the 'ands of God. I thought about it, you know, thar at the wheel, and I says to meself, 'e's not wrong about that. *(Warming to his theme.)* You know, sometimes a pot just goes wrong and I have to stop, roll it back into a ball and start again. Often the second time round, the pot is perfect!

JERRY: *(Clearly exasperated by the lack of drama in this story.)* Well, there you have it, folks. Jeremiah watched Mr Potter at work and thought he heard God speaking to him. Judah isn't keen to listen to him and frankly I'm not surprised! But what do you think? You decide!

(Audience applause, show ends, all leave the stage except Jeremiah.)

JEREMIAH: *(Looking up.)* I'm sorry. I tried, I really did. (Jeremiah gets up and dejectedly walks off stage.)

Enough evidence to convict you?

If you were put on trial for your beliefs, would there be enough evidence to convict you?

Have a look at the statements below. If you think that the activity is something that it is OK for a Christian to do, tick 'OK'. If you think a Christian shouldn't do it, tick 'Not OK'. Be ready to give a reason for your answer!

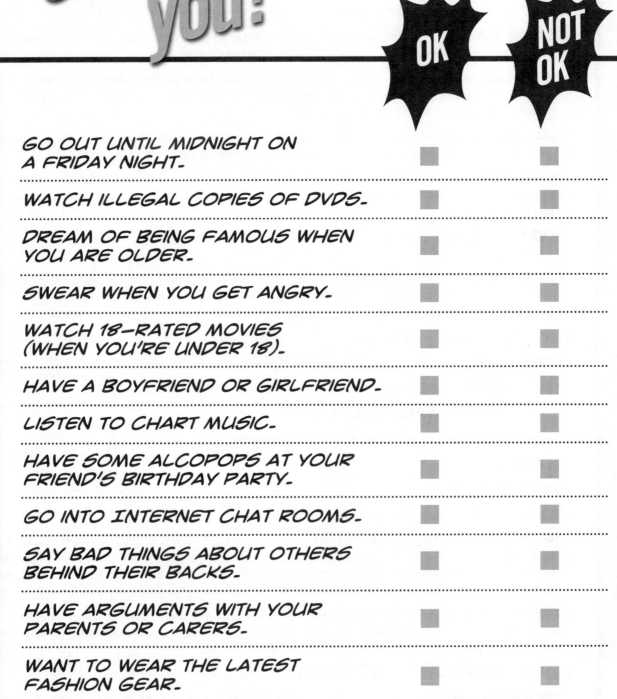

	OK	NOT OK
GO OUT UNTIL MIDNIGHT ON A FRIDAY NIGHT.	☐	☐
WATCH ILLEGAL COPIES OF DVDS.	☐	☐
DREAM OF BEING FAMOUS WHEN YOU ARE OLDER.	☐	☐
SWEAR WHEN YOU GET ANGRY.	☐	☐
WATCH 18–RATED MOVIES (WHEN YOU'RE UNDER 18).	☐	☐
HAVE A BOYFRIEND OR GIRLFRIEND.	☐	☐
LISTEN TO CHART MUSIC.	☐	☐
HAVE SOME ALCOPOPS AT YOUR FRIEND'S BIRTHDAY PARTY.	☐	☐
GO INTO INTERNET CHAT ROOMS.	☐	☐
SAY BAD THINGS ABOUT OTHERS BEHIND THEIR BACKS.	☐	☐
HAVE ARGUMENTS WITH YOUR PARENTS OR CARERS.	☐	☐
WANT TO WEAR THE LATEST FASHION GEAR.	☐	☐

The coming of Jesus

THESE PASSAGES FROM THE START OF THE GOSPELS REPRESENT A TURNING POINT IN THE STORY OF SALVATION – GOD'S PEOPLE HAVE TO WAIT NO LONGER; THE MESSIAH, PROMISED BY THE PROPHET ISAIAH AND OTHERS, HAS COME TO SAVE THE WORLD. THE EVENTS OF THE OLD TESTAMENT POINT TOWARDS JESUS, AND HIS ACTIONS, DEATH AND RESURRECTION WILL HAVE AN EVERLASTING IMPACT ON THE WORLD.

The Christmas stories will be pretty well known, but even church young people will have trouble sorting out what is mere tradition from the narrative as Matthew and Luke describe it. It is an interesting path to take to challenge all young people on what the Christmas story is actually about, sifting out donkeys and Santa and reindeer and robins. What does the Christmas story mean to you?

You might see the other stories in this section, together with the Christmas narratives, as the Gospel writers introducing Jesus and his ministry. He is born; the wise men's gifts tell us of what Jesus will be; John baptises Jesus and God is present there; Jesus prepares himself in the desert; Jesus selects his disciples, announcing to them in ways that spoke clearly to them.

FOR THOSE FROM OUTSIDE A CHURCH COMMUNITY
If you're starting a group by using these passages, this may well be the first time that young people with no church background have heard about Jesus. They will be familiar with Christmas, but perhaps not the real story behind it. Use this as a way into thinking about the real meaning of these stories. The other stories in this section make an effective introduction to Jesus and why he came. There are some strange events here which are likely to bring lots of questions. Make sure you have reflected on these Bible passages yourself before exploring them with your group.

FOR THOSE WITH A CHURCH BACKGROUND
Christmas is familiar, maybe too familiar for many young people who have grown up in church. Take some time to look at the Christmas narrative in the context of the wider story of the Bible. The wise men's gifts may be particularly effective in doing this. Most church young people know what the gifts are, but perhaps not what they might represent. Use this whole section to gauge what the young people know and think about Jesus – what is their relationship with him?

GOD IN THE FLESH

LUKE 2:1–21

31

WHAT: *Nativity play*
WHY: *To see that God is faithful by sending Jesus*
WITH: *Bibles, simple first-century costumes and appropriate props (optional)*

1   Gather the group together and ask them if they can remember the last time they were in a nativity play. Is there anyone who longed to be Mary or Joseph, but never got the chance? Tell everyone that they're going to get another chance to be in a nativity!

2   Read the Bible passage: **Luke 2:1–21**. A leader or young person could read this.

3   Challenge the young people to plan out the play and decide who will take which parts. Make sure the young people cover this session's Bible passage accurately! Get them to rehearse and then perform it. If your group is not happy to ad-lib then they could act while a leader tells the story.

4   When you have finished, discuss what the story is actually about, behind the familiar elements of the innkeeper, shepherds and angels. What relevance does this story have to them? Is it more than just a story? If appropriate, challenge the young people to think about the significance of Jesus' birth.

STARS IN THEIR EYES

MATTHEW 2:1–23

32

WHAT: *Route planner*
WHY: *To discover that God comes to all people*
WITH: *Bibles, old magazines, scissors, backing paper, glue sticks, a world atlas*

1   Provide the group with a selection of magazines and invite them to cut out faces from as many different ethnic backgrounds as possible. Then ask the young people to make a collage of these faces.

2   Ask the group to discuss what the statement, 'Jesus comes to all people' means to them.

3   Read **Matthew 2:1–23** and ask the young people to make a note of all the different places that are mentioned and the journeys made. Identify these places and journeys on a world atlas and help the young people to grasp the length of journeys involved.

4   Ask a few volunteers to tell the group about the longest journey they have ever made.

5   Encourage the group to think about the journey made by the wise men. They travelled a long way!

Ask:
• Why do you think they were prepared to do this?
• What sort of sacrifices might they have had to make in order to undertake this journey?

Ask the group to consider what they are prepared to do to 'meet with Jesus' and what are some of the sacrifices they might have to make.

6   Conclude by explaining that the good news of the gospel is not that we have to make a long journey to Jesus, but that Jesus made a long journey to us – he came from heaven to live among us. And he made it possible for all people to know him personally.

EARMARKED

MATTHEW 3:1–17

33

WHAT: *Quiz and discussion*
WHY: *To explore how God equips his people through the Spirit*
WITH: *Bibles, paper, pens, copies of 'Symbols' resource sheet from page 48*

1. Divide the young people into four groups and allocate each group one of the following characters: John; Jesus; Pharisees and Sadducees; the Holy Spirit.

2. Get each group to read **Matthew 3:1–17** together and, as they do, they should make notes about what they learn about their character. What opinions are expressed about them and how are they described?

3. Gather the group together and find out their thoughts. Then, explain to the group that these events took place just before Jesus started his public ministry – they were a significant part of his preparation. Say that many churches still baptise people today and ask why, according to verse 11, might baptism be an important part of equipping and preparing Christians?

4. Give out copies of the 'Symbols' resource sheet and challenge everyone to complete the symbols quiz.

5. Next, ask the young people to look at the symbols further down the page. Explain that they are all symbols that relate to the Holy Spirit. In small groups, get them to discuss how the Holy Spirit is like each of them. The Bible verses might help. (Please note that some of the verses don't relate directly to the Holy Spirit; however, they show what these symbols often represent in the Bible.)

6. Bring the group together and find out how they think the symbols relate to the Holy Spirit. Conclude by discussing how they think the Holy Spirit prepares and equips people today.

BE PREPARED

MATTHEW 4:1–11

34

WHAT: *Watch and chat*
WHY: *To be better equipped to go God's way rather than the easy route*
WITH: *TV and DVD player or laptop and projector, 'How far would you go?' resource sheet from page 47*

1. Watch a short clip from a TV show such as *I'm a Celebrity…* or *Bansai*, where people have to take part in a horrible challenge in order to win a prize for themselves or someone else. (Check that the clip doesn't contain offensive language or behaviour.) Ask the group what they think motivates the contestants in shows like these.

2. In pairs or threes, invite the group to read the 'How far would you go?' resource sheet. Encourage them to discuss the questions: 'Do you think you would be able to do the things that those real-life stories show? Why, or why not?'

3. Now read **Matthew 4:1–11** aloud to the group. Work out together exactly how Jesus was challenged, in what was certainly no game show. (There was: a physical challenge involving food; a psychological challenge about Jesus proving who he was; and a spiritual challenge about giving in and worshipping the devil.)

4. Discuss why Jesus stood up to these temptations – what did he 'win' by doing so? Each of these would have been the easy, selfish route for him to take. Jesus was determined not to misuse his power and authority but to do things God's way.

FOLLOW

LUKE 5:1–11, 27–32

WHAT: *Questionnaire and discussion*
WHY: *To discover that Jesus challenges us to follow him*
WITH: *'Numero uno' questionnaire from page 49, pens, Bibles*

1 Make sure everyone has a copy of the 'Numero uno' questionnaire. When everyone has finished it, divide the young people into small groups and encourage them to discuss their responses and chat about their chosen priorities.

2 Ask a volunteer to read **Luke 5:1–11, 27–32** aloud and discuss together what they think Jesus meant when he told Peter and the others to 'follow him'? If you like, you could introduce this discussion by providing them with these options:

a) He was inviting them to join him in a quick game of 'follow my leader'.

b) He had something exciting round the corner that they just had to see.

c) He was offering them a better career with more pay (apparently there's more money in catching people than fish!).

d) Something else…

3 Explain to the group that when Jesus said 'follow me' he was basically asking them to make him and his mission their 'Numero Uno' – their top priority. Ask the group what this would have meant for the fishermen and Levi, for example in terms of their ambitions, jobs, families, or where they lived.

4 Ask the young people to look back at the 'Numero Uno' questionnaire and think about what option they think Jesus would want them to choose in each of these situations.

5 Encourage everyone to spend a few moments thinking about how their life would be different if Jesus and his mission was their top priority, their 'Numero Uno'.

HERE ARE SOME TRUE STORIES FROM AROUND THE WORLD. SOME OF THEM DESCRIBE THINGS PEOPLE DID FOR THEIR FAITH, OTHERS SHOW THINGS PEOPLE DID FOR OTHERS — FAMILY, FRIENDS AND STRANGERS. THINK ABOUT WHAT THEY GAVE UP. THINK ABOUT WHY THEY DID IT. THINK ABOUT HOW FAR YOU WOULD GO TO HELP SOMEONE ELSE, OR TO STAND UP FOR WHAT YOU BELIEVE IN.

HOW FAR WOULD YOU GO?

WWII

During World War II, a Dutch family called ten Boom helped Jewish families escape from the Nazis. There were some families who could not be smuggled out, and they stayed in the ten Boom family house in Harlem, Holland. The Nazis were tipped off, and the ten Boom family was arrested and sent to concentration camps. The Nazis did not find the hidden Jews, who were smuggled away to safety. The ten Boom family suffered greatly in the concentration camp and only one daughter, called Corrie, survived. After the war, she helped with work to reconcile former enemies.

VANISHED

In El Salvador, the military Junta carried out a systematic programme to wipe out their political enemies. These people, 'the disappeared', would vanish from the street. Often they were never found again. Sometimes a body would be found showing signs of torture. Most of the population was too scared to say anything against the rulers. However, the Catholic Bishop, Oscar Romero, frequently preached peace from his pulpit, and condemned the work of the soldiers and hit squads. One Sunday, as he was celebrating Mass, soldiers burst into the cathedral and shot him.

CHARITY

Sue Ryder worked with the Special Operations Executive (SOE) during WWII. This was the forerunner of MI6. After the war, she continued to work in Europe with displaced people – those who had been forced to move or had fled fighting, and now had nowhere to return to. She helped supply food, clothing, shelter, medical aid and training. Eventually, the only people left in her care were those too frail, too ill, or too disabled to work to support themselves. Sue Ryder set up a charity, which still works throughout Europe and the UK to provide care and accommodation to those unable to live independently.

RUSSIA

In the Soviet Union, there was heavy censorship on all creative arts, especially writing. A poet called Irina Ratushinskaya, who was a Christian, carried on writing freely. She was sentenced to twelve years in a prison camp for 'anti-Soviet agitation in the form of poetry'. Whilst there, she was put in solitary confinement without food or water. She stayed alive by licking condensation off the metal door to her cell. She was also badly beaten by the guards on a regular basis. When she was released, she forgave the guards.

EXTRAORDINARY

In **Matthew 4:1–11** *Jesus said 'no' to doing things the devil's way and 'yes' to doing things God's way, and that wasn't easy. In these stories the people are resisting the temptation of an easier life, choosing to do the hard thing, God's way. The people involved would all describe themselves as ordinary people. Yet, they managed extraordinary things. We are also ordinary people. Do you think, with God's help, you could do extraordinary things?*

Symbols

Holy Spirit symbols

Here are some common symbols that are used to represent and describe the Holy Spirit. How do you think the Holy Spirit is like these things?

WATER

PSALM 51:7-11;
EZEKIEL 36:25-27

WIND

JOHN 3:8;
ACTS 2:2

FIRE

ACTS 2:3;
ZECHARIAH 13:9

DOVE

MATTHEW 3:16;
MATTHEW 10:16

SEAL

EPHESIANS 1:13,14

Numero Uno

Have you ever tried to answer some of those 'Would you rather...' questions? Questions like 'Would you rather have an Indian or Chinese takeaway?' or 'Would you rather break your arm or your leg?' Well, these questions are a bit like that, just a bit more challenging! Just so you know, you're not allowed to sit on the fence and no telling fibs to make yourself look better. Be honest!

BRAND NEW TOP OF THE RANGE TRAINERS	OR	FAIRLY TRADED TRAINERS FROM OXFAM
KEEPING QUIET WHILE YOUR MATES MAKE RACIST COMMENTS	OR	TELLING YOUR MATES YOU THINK THEY ARE WRONG TO BE RACIST
PUTTING £10 IN THE COLLECTION AT CHURCH	OR	SPENDING £10 TO TOP UP YOUR PHONE CREDIT
REFUSING TO WATCH A 15-RATED FILM WITH YOUR MATES	OR	WATCHING THE FILM AT THE CINEMA AND LYING ABOUT YOUR AGE
HELPING YOUR FRIEND OUT WITH THEIR MATHS REVISION	OR	PLAYING A VIDEO GAME WITH ANOTHER FRIEND
HANGING OUT WITH YOUR MATES AT BREAK	OR	MAKING FRIENDS WITH SOMEONE WHO'S ON THEIR OWN
HAVE A DRINK WITH ALL YOUR MATES AT THE PARTY	OR	BE THE ONLY ONE AT THE PARTY WHO DOESN'T DRINK ALCOHOL
TIDYING YOUR BEDROOM	OR	LEAVING IT A TIP
MAKE TIME TO WATCH YOUR FAVOURITE SOAPS ON TV	OR	MAKE TIME TO READ YOUR BIBLE
CUT THE GRASS	OR	HAVE A LIE-IN

Jesus in action

DULL – A WORD THAT YOU COULD NEVER APPLY TO JESUS. TO ANY YOUNG PERSON, REGARDLESS OF BACKGROUND, THE STORIES IN THIS SECTION WILL SEEM STRANGE, OTHER-WORLDLY, MORE SUITED TO FANTASY FICTION OR VIDEO GAMES THAN TO A BOOK LIKE THE BIBLE. YET, IN CARRYING OUT GOD'S PURPOSES, JESUS NEVER SHIRKS FROM THE UNEXPECTED OR DIFFICULT. CASTING OUT DEMONS, BRINGING A GIRL BACK FROM THE DEAD, CALMING A STORM, FEEDING OVER 5,000 PEOPLE AND TEACHING THAT TURNS THE WORLD ON ITS HEAD – ALL OF THESE THINGS WOULD HAVE BEEN RADICAL, AWE-INSPIRING AND EVEN UNSETTLING FOR THOSE WHO SAW IT ALL FIRST HAND. HOW MUCH MORE SO WILL THESE EVENTS BE TO OUR YOUNG PEOPLE?

Be careful not to sensationalise the supernatural, otherwise you run the risk of turning Jesus' actions into just another fantasy story. Instead, use these events to challenge the young people's view of Jesus. What do these stories tell us about Jesus' character and mission? Give the young people a chance to explore how these events relate to the larger story of the Bible – the Jews were expecting a hero to save them from occupation by the Romans, but here Jesus is demonstrating his divinity and Lordship over all of creation, not just the Roman Empire.

FOR THOSE FROM OUTSIDE A CHURCH COMMUNITY
For young people with little or no knowledge of Jesus, these stories are going to be revelatory. Any ideas of a dull Jesus are blown away by his radical actions! Foster a sense of wonder and discovery as you explore these passages, using the activity on the Lord's prayer to reflect back on the other narratives of this section – if Jesus is like this, then what is our response to that?

FOR THOSE WITH A CHURCH BACKGROUND
It might be worth spending some time talking about the young people's current picture of Jesus before you look at the narratives in this section – you could create a social network profile for him and use this to explore attitudes to him and his actions. Then, as you read through these stories of Jesus in action, continue adding in new information to the profile. How do Jesus' actions challenge these ideas of what he is like and what he came to do?

IN SICKNESS AND IN HEALTH

MARK 1:29–34

36

WHAT: *Physical activity and discussion*
WHY: *To celebrate that Jesus is Lord over demons and sickness*
WITH: *Bibles*

1 In advance, think up a list of some activities that are possible for your young people to do themselves, some that they might be able to do with lots of practise or hard work, and some that are impossible for normal people to do. For example: getting 100 per cent in their Maths test, flying a kite in a force 10 gale, doing a bungee jump or lifting the lightest person in the group single-handed. Include 'touching someone to make them well' as one of the activities in the list. (Obviously, they won't be required to prove they can do any of these!) Designate three areas of the room for 'definitely possible', 'maybe possible' and 'definitely impossible'.

2 Explain to the group that you are going to read out various situations and they need to respond by moving to the appropriate part of the room, depending on whether they think they could do each of the activities themselves. Don't spend too long on this activity and keep it fast moving.

3 When you've finished, gather the group together and read **Mark 1:29–34** to the group, preferably from a modern paraphrased Bible such as The Dramatised Bible or The Message.

4 In smaller groups, ask them to discuss why they think it was possible for Jesus to heal the sick and drive out demons. Did it seem to be a difficult task for him?

5 Leave them with the thought that Christians believe that Jesus could heal people who had sicknesses and demons because he was God in human form. When you have power over something, it can be said that you are 'lord' over it. Jesus is Lord over sickness and demons, because he has power over them.

DON'T FEAR THE REAPER

MARK 5:21–43

37

WHAT: *Re-creation*
WHY: *To rejoice that Jesus is Lord over death*

1 Introduce this contemporary scenario: A young girl has died. Her body is still in the house. The undertakers have not yet arrived. A man you know, vaguely, arrives at the door. You ask him why he is here. He says, 'She's not dead, only sleeping.'

2 Breaking into smaller groups, if necessary, encourage everyone to plan how the scene now develops as people react to this apparently tactless statement. Get them to think about the characters in the situation: How do the parents react? What about close friends? Is there a doctor there?

3 Get feedback, then ask: 'What happened next?' It would be good if the group could act out the situation in a role-play format.

4 Now tell the story of Jesus raising the dead girl in **Mark 5:21–23, 35–43**. Omit the interruption from the woman with the haemorrhaging.

5 Comparing this Bible episode with their role-play situation, ask if the young people would have trusted Jesus if he had said that about their daughter or if they would have thrown him out. Is there anything different between the contemporary situation and the story in the Bible? What you're looking for is the fact that Jairus asked Jesus for help and he had faith that his daughter would be OK. And she was, because Jesus is Lord over death.

IN DANGER!

MATTHEW 8:23–27

38

WHAT: *Reflect*
WHY: *To discover more about our powerful God and to explore our response to him*
WITH: *Bibles,* Oriel's Diary *by Robert Harrison (optional), recording equipment (optional)*

1 Ask the group to imagine they are one of the disciples. They will need to focus on the feelings of the disciples and try to understand how afraid they were – remember that they were experienced fishermen.

2 Invite a good reader to read out **Matthew 8:23–27**.

3 Alternatively, you could read the 'fictitious' account from *Oriel's Diary*. (If you do this, read the version from the Bible afterwards.)

4 Divide into groups and discuss:

• What might be the modern equivalent of that scary, out-of-control situation where it seemed that all hope was lost?
• How would the people involved react?

5 Ask the groups to act out their situations. It's always fun to video the scenes, but check your church's child protection policy on parental permission first.

6 Bring the groups together and invite them to share their situations. Ask:
• How are these new situations similar or different to the original story?
• What was the disciples' response to Jesus in both the original setting and in their modern improvisation?
• How would you have responded to what Jesus did?

THE BREAD OF LIFE

JOHN 6:1–15, 25–40

39

WHAT: *Sketch and discussion*
WHY: *To discover that Jesus offers us eternal life*
WITH: *Bibles, copies of John 6:25–40, pens, copies of 'See, come, believe' script from page 54*

1 Divide the young people into groups of about three. In their group, invite them to read **John 6:1–15** and discuss why Jesus performed this miracle and what they can learn about Jesus from it.

2 Gather everyone back together and encourage each group to feed back. Then, explain to the young people that Jesus' miracles not only helped people, they revealed God's power and he often used them as illustrations to make a spiritual point. (As an example, refer to an illustration you've used with the group recently and explain that Jesus' illustrations were just somewhat more impressive than yours!) In this session, they'll discover that after Jesus had fed the people with 'physical' bread, he went on to talk about 'spiritual' bread.

3 Hand out copies of **John 6:25–40** and ask a few volunteers to read it. While the passage is being read, suggest that the young people underline bits they find confusing or strange.

4 Now ask three young people to act out the 'See, come, believe' sketch.

5 Have a chat about the sketch. Encourage the young people to express their opinions about the different characters and what they were saying. Also discuss the parts of the passage they underlined earlier.

6 Finish by concluding that Jesus had provided for the people's physical needs by feeding them (in the feeding of the 5,000). He was now saying that he could meet a greater need. See if the group can identify what that greater need was.

TEACH ME TO PRAY

LUKE 11:1–4;
MATTHEW 6:5–15

40

WHAT: Game
WHY: To discover how Jesus wants us to pray
WITH: Bible, questions below written on a flip chart or copied out for the group to see

1   Get the young people to think of one thing they have been taught that will never be useful to them, for example quadratic equations, philosophical theories or knitting. Suggest that they prepare a brief argument to support their opinion. They could do this activity in pairs and feed back to everyone.

2   Invite a confident reader to read **Luke 11:1–4** to the group. Say that here the disciples are asking Jesus to teach them something that is useful for everyone.

3   Ask another young person to read **Matthew 6:5–15**.

4   In their pairs, ask them to discuss these questions (write them on the flip chart before the session):
• Why did Jesus make prayer such a priority?
• What did he gain from it?
• What attitudes did he encourage when praying?

5   Invite everyone to share their answers.

KNOCK ON THE DOOR

LUKE 11:5–13

41

WHAT: Drama
WHY: To be inspired to talk with God in the way he wants us to
WITH: Copies of 'Your need, we supply' script from page 57

1   Give a copy of the 'Your need, we supply' script to each person and get them to read the script. Or you could ask a few young people to prepare the sketch and perform it to the rest of the group.

2   Afterwards, challenge the group to list other things that are easily confused.

3   Tell the group that Jesus told his followers what they should do when they needed something. He told them they should talk to God in prayer, but he also gave them some guidelines on how they should pray.

4   Ask a good reader to read **Luke 11:5–13**, and as the passage is being read ask the rest of the group to list what it is telling them about how to pray.

5   Ask the group what they came up with. Make sure that they have realised that they should ask God for what they need, be persistent and bold (honest), and trust that God will not give us what we don't need – unlike the new agency in the play.

See, come, believe

THE CHARACTERS

MR SMART-SPEAK: INTELLECTUAL-LOOKING RE TEACHER

JASMIN: TALKATIVE, STREET WISE 13-YEAR-OLD

SIMON: QUESTIONING, SHY, 13-YEAR-OLD (QUITE LIKES JASMIN!)

Scene: classroom

MR SMART-SPEAK: So you see, class, in this passage Jesus says he is the bread that gives life. *(Jasmin sniggers.)*

JASMIN: *(Mumbling under her breath.)* Yeah, right, how can a man be bread that gives life? Stupid idea if ever I heard one. Even McDonald's don't claim that. And what if you have a wheat allergy? Bread's no good then.

MR SMART-SPEAK: *(Authoritatively.)* No, he is using something called an 'analogy'. For example, you need bread to be able to live – *(Almost irritated but not quite.)* or other food if you have a gluten intolerance – so Jesus is saying that just as bread is essential to life, he is essential for eternal life. *(Simon puts his hand up to ask a question.)*

SIMON: Excuse me, Sir, but this is really complicated. Am I right in thinking that you're saying that this Jesus, who we can't actually see, says that if we come to him and believe in him, we'll have life for ever? *(Jasmin giggles and mimics Simon, who looks affronted.)*

MR SMART-SPEAK: Exactly Simon, not easy to understand, I appreciate. In fact, down through history, just like the Jews in this story, people have had difficulty in getting their heads round it... *(Gets ready to launch into a history lesson.)*

JASMIN: *(Interrupting.)* So, Sir, you're saying that this Jesus bloke, who did loads of miracles and fed five thousand people, can also help us have eternal life, just like he gave those people bread? Cool dude! That's what I say! I fancy having eternal life, with coke and fries – in fact supersize! *(Starts singing 'I'm gonna live forever' from Fame.)*

SIMON: *(Turning to Jasmin.)* I can't believe that it's that simple!

JASMIN: Well, that's what Sir read earlier, that if we come to this Jesus, say we're sorry, try to do better and believe in him, he's gonna be with us now and for ever. *(At this point, Jasmin and Simon strike up their own conversation on this subject while Mr Smart-Speak strives to get the class in order!)*

MR SMART-SPEAK: *(Bell rings.)* Right class, gather up your books and we'll look at this some more tomorrow, unless of course you want to read it again to see for yourself? You'll find it all in **John 6:25–40**.

Your need, we supply!

An official is sitting behind a desk. They have a pen, several sheets of paper and a computer. The first person enters the room, dressed in builders' clothes, and sits down opposite the official.

OFFICIAL: Good morning and welcome to Your Need; We Supply, a new government agency here to help those with needs. Your name?

GORDON CAMERON: Gordon Cameron.

OFFICIAL: Thank you. I have your file here and I am pleased to tell you that we can help you. Could you just explain again your situation and what exactly you need from us?

GORDON CAMERON: Well, I recently lost my job because the company I was working for went bankrupt. I have been looking for similar work…

OFFICIAL: And that is in the building industry, isn't it?

GORDON CAMERON: Yes, I am a builder by trade and I am especially good at plastering, but I am multi-skilled – carpentry, stonework – you name it, I can do it. Well, I have been looking for work and I have now found a job. I start next Monday, but I won't get paid for a month and so I am very short at the moment and need something to tide me over. So what I need from you is a monkey.

(The official looks startled.)

OFFICIAL: A monkey?

GORDON CAMERON: Yeah, that should do, I am sure that is all I need and will help me get by.

OFFICIAL: Right, OK, well I'll note that down and if you wait outside it'll be brought along to you in a short time.

(The official types on the computer.)

GORDON CAMERON: Great, that's wonderful, thanks, you're the salt of the earth, great geezer.

OFFICIAL: Next!

(A second person enters the room as Gordon Cameron leaves. They are dressed in bright colours and bounce into the room in a dreamy way.)

OFFICIAL: Good morning and how can we help you?

EMILY STRANGE: Hi, my name's Emily Strange. This is a really cool idea, man, giving to people in need. That's right on.

OFFICIAL: Right, well I am glad that you approve of our little agency. How can we help?

EMILY STRANGE: Well, I have been trying to start my own business, selling tie-dyed Wellington boots. They are really cool looking and I have already got plenty of advance orders for them. But I have run out of dye and I can't complete the order.

OFFICIAL: Right, so what do you need?

EMILY STRANGE: Well, I simply need some bread to sort things out.

(Again, the official looks puzzled.)

OFFICIAL: Bread?

EMILY STRANGE: Yeah, bread man.

OFFICIAL: (Still looking puzzled.) Well, OK then, if you wait outside I'll get some 'bread' out to you. (The official again types into his computer. Emily leaves as Gordon comes back in.)

GORDON CAMERON: Have you lost your mind?

OFFICIAL: Sorry? What is the problem?

GORDON CAMERON: I've just been attacked by some crazy Proboscis monkey! Are you out of your head?

OFFICIAL: What do you mean? I ordered and got what you asked for. You said you needed a monkey and that is what I gave you.

GORDON CAMERON: Yeah, I said a monkey but that means £500 where I come from. It was the money that I needed.

OFFICIAL: Well, why didn't you say that? If you want something you should clearly ask for what it is.

GORDON CAMERON: Perhaps this wasn't such a good idea.

(Gordon Cameron leaves and Emily Strange enters the room.)

EMILY STRANGE: What am I going to do with several boxes of 'Stay fresh for a week' wholemeal loaves? I am trying to make hippy boots not open a sandwich shop.

OFFICIAL: You asked for bread!

Emily Strange: Yeah, I asked for bread because that is what I call money. I needed money to buy the dye!

OFFICIAL: Oh, I see, well you should have been clear too. You can't say one thing and mean another. How was I to know you need money when you asked for bread?

(Emily Strange leaves, obviously frustrated.)

OFFICIAL: People are strange. They never say what they mean.

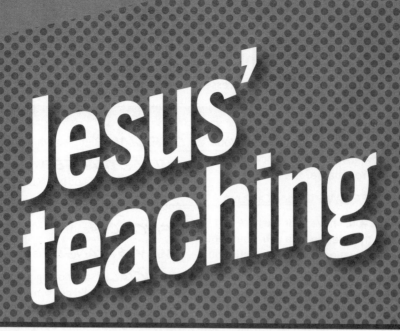

Jesus' teaching

LIKE HIS ACTIONS AND MIRACLES, JESUS' TEACHING IS DYNAMIC AND ENGAGING, MAKING USE OF STORIES, PARABLES, MEMORABLE SAYINGS, THE ENVIRONMENT IN WHICH HE TAUGHT. IN IT, HE TURNS THE ORDER OF THINGS UPSIDE DOWN AND CONFOUNDS THE EXPECTATIONS OF HIS LISTENERS. SOMETIMES, HIS WORDS ARE EVEN SHOCKING IN THEIR RADICAL NATURE. BUT ALL THESE THINGS TELL US MORE AND MORE ABOUT JESUS' MISSION AND HOW GOD IS MOVING TO BRING ABOUT THE SALVATION OF HIS PEOPLE.

The nature of Jesus' words are challenging to young people. He calls us to put God first, and yet our world is increasingly individualistic. Jesus' call to love God and love our neighbours as ourselves (see the story of the good Samaritan) lies at the heart of the kingdom. We must seek to love others, not out of some legalistic compulsion, but out of love for God.

Martin Luther King once preached on the story of the good Samaritan and said this: 'The first question the priest and the Levite asked themselves was "If I stop to help this man, what will happen to me?" The Samaritan came by and reversed the question, "If I do not stop to help this man, what will happen to him?"' How can we help young people to catch the vision of Jesus' kingdom calling?

FOR THOSE FROM OUTSIDE A CHURCH COMMUNITY

These 'well-known' stories may be unknown to young people with limited church background, yet they have the potential to be explosive! Jesus' call is so countercultural that his priorities may well be difficult for young people to process. Questions about helping others with no thought of reward, of placing others before yourself, of comforting those who are distressed regardless of who they are will all be thrown up. Then there is the question of accepting God's forgiveness, whatever we have done, in the story of the lost son. This may be the most difficult of all to process. With sensitivity, help young people think more deeply about the implications of this.

FOR THOSE WITH A CHURCH BACKGROUND

Young people from a church community will probably know these parables and the Beatitudes, but you may be surprised about their level of understanding of what Jesus is saying. Help these young people come back to these passages with open minds and discover afresh what Jesus is saying. How do his words affect their faith? What does it say about God's priorities? What does that mean for our walk with him?

BAD ATTITUDE

MATTHEW 5:1–12

42

WHAT: *Create a city*
WHY: *To challenge the world's view with God's view*
WITH: *Large sheet of paper (brown paper is good for this), felt-tip pens, newspapers and magazines, scissors, glue sticks (optional)*

1 Divide your young people into two groups. Give the first group the large sheet of paper and felt-tip pens. Their task is to work together to design their ideal city. They should begin by laying out natural features (mountains, rivers, lakes, forests) and then add in roads or other transportation routes, then finally buildings and housing. Encourage them to think about what makes a city a good place to live and to design it accordingly.

2 Give the second group a selection of current newspapers and magazines, and a list of the following types of people: poor, homeless, hungry, lost, sad, diseased, depressed, lonely, unemployed, orphaned, widowed. Ask them to find pictures of people who fit the descriptions and cut them out.

3 When both groups are ready, bring them together. Encourage group one to talk about their city.

4 Invite the second group to bring their people images and choose the best places for them to live in the city. If you have time, the images could be stuck in place.

5 Invite a short discussion. Can the group imagine anything like this happening in the world today? Do the poor usually even get a choice where they live? Is this fair?

6 Explain that the picture they have made is a little like the new world that Jesus spoke of in **Matthew 5:1–12** when he said, amongst other things, 'those who are humble are happy, because the earth will belong to them'. Jesus was talking about how God's view of the world is different to ours. Normally in the world, the richest and boldest people often do well, and get the nice houses. In our city map it was the poor and underprivileged who had the choice. If you like you could invite the young people to rewrite Jesus' words in their own words as the title of their picture.

7 Read **Matthew 5:1–12** to the group. After each verse ask them why what Jesus is suggesting is different to what happens normally in the world.

WE ARE THE ONE

JOHN 14:1–14

43

WHAT: *Game*
WHY: *To discover that Jesus and the Father are one*
WITH: *Sheets of paper, pens, container, stopwatch, Bibles*

1 Give everyone four sheets of paper and a pen. They need to write down the names of four people – one on each piece – fold them up and put them in the container. They should be names of people that everyone has heard of.

2 Divide the group into two teams. One person from a team picks a piece of paper out of the container and has to get the rest of his or her team to guess the name on it by giving them clues. As soon as the name is guessed correctly, they draw another piece of paper. Give them one minute to see how many their team can guess correctly.

3 Summarise by saying that they may be able to guess who someone is in the name game, but does that mean they know them?

4 Get the group to think about people that they know well. Discuss: How did you get to know them? How long did it take? What would help you get to know someone better?

5 Explain that the disciples asked Jesus how they could get to know God, his Father. Philip, one of the disciples, said, 'Show us the Father. That is all we need.' And Jesus said something quite amazing.

6 Make sure everyone can see a Bible and read **John 14:9–11** together. Discuss the following questions:
• How did Jesus say they could know his Father? (By looking at Jesus, v 9.)
• This is quite an amazing thing to believe. What evidence did Jesus say they have to prove it was true? (The miracles he performed, v 11.) How would that help them believe?
• What does it mean to us that Jesus and his Father are one?

ARE YOU SITTING COMFORTABLY?

LUKE 10:25–37

WHAT: *Personal stories*
WHY: *To experience the power of a story that could change our life*
WITH: *Bibles, paper, pens*

1 Get everyone to sit in a circle and ask if anyone has ever been rescued. Get the young people to tell their stories and answer questions. Give two or three people a chance to do this.

2 Brainstorm, 'If you were stuck, who would you like to be rescued by?' Next think about, 'Who would you least like to be rescued by, and why?' As an example, get everyone to imagine being stuck in a place they had been forbidden to visit (such as a shed on an allotment where the door banged and was stuck shut) and then being rescued by a frantic and worried parent some hours later with 'I told you not to...' Explain that you would be happy to be rescued but sad to be caught being disobedient. Ask the young people to think of and share other examples.

3 Read or retell the story of the good Samaritan from **Luke 10:25–37**. The version in The Message is particularly strong.

4 Explain why the Samaritan was the last person in the world that the hearers of the story would have expected to be the rescuer (although the rescued man himself was probably happy to be rescued by anyone by this time!).

5 Encourage the young people each to think about and write on a small piece of paper the name of a person or group they find hard to love or imagine being friends with. This prejudice may be undeserved or not. Assure them that the papers will be treated anonymously.

6 Collect the papers and lay them down on the floor in the shape of a cross. Read **John 3:16** to remind everyone that God loved the world without any hint of prejudice. Anyone can come to Jesus. That's the way Christians should love too.

ADMIT ONE

LUKE 14:15–24

WHAT: *Discussion*
WHY: *To recognise that the invitation from Jesus is for all people*
WITH: *Bibles*

1 Read out the following list of people and ask the young people to decide, in pairs, who they would allow into heaven and why: bank robber, murderer, school teacher, church leader, nurse, drug dealer, pop star, TV celebrity (you may add to this list if you want to make it more topical).

2 In one group, encourage the young people to share some of the things they have discussed. Ask:
• Who have you decided should be allowed into heaven?
• How did you make your decision?

3 Read or ask a good reader to read **Luke 14:15–24**. Ask the group:
• Who was supposed to come to the banquet?
• Who came in the end?
• How many people were invited in the end?

4 Talk about what the banquet symbolises (heaven) and who the man, or master, in the passage represents (God). What does this Bible passage say about the group's earlier decisions about who gets into heaven and who doesn't? Do they want to change their minds? Highlight that Jesus invites everyone into heaven, and it's up to us to accept the invitation. It's not about who we are or what we have done.

WHATEVER I'VE DONE?

LUKE 15:11–32

46

WHAT: *Role play*
WHY: *To realise that we can all receive God's undeserved forgiveness*

1 Read **Luke 15:11–32** aloud to the young people, or get a confident young person to read it.

2 In groups, give the young people ten minutes to create their own modern-day drama or role play based on the passage. If they are struggling, suggest these:

A girl mixes with the 'wrong' crowd. She is warned by her parents that her friends are always in trouble, which will affect the way she lives. She becomes pregnant, and then runs away. She lives rough for a while and then realises that at home with her parents, she was at least warm and well fed. She decides to return... How does the story turn out? (This works best with an older group.)

A boy gets heavily into gaming. He spends more and more time gaming online and as a result his grades at school begin to slip. He pesters his parents for the latest games but when they won't give in, he steals the money to buy an 'N-Gage' game, which is pants. Because of stealing the money he can't go on a school trip to a theme park. Then he asks to be forgiven... How does this story turn out?

One young person goes to a rock concert with their friends, despite being told not to. Meanwhile their sibling obeys the parents and stays at home. When the other child returns they say that they are sorry and are taken out for a meal at Pizza Hut... How does this turn out? What are the feelings of the child who did what they were told?

3 Invite the groups to present their dramas or role plays.

4 Chat through the following questions with the young people:
  • Why did you end the dramas or role plays the way you did?
  • How deserving of forgiveness were the characters?
  • What does this say about the way God forgives people?

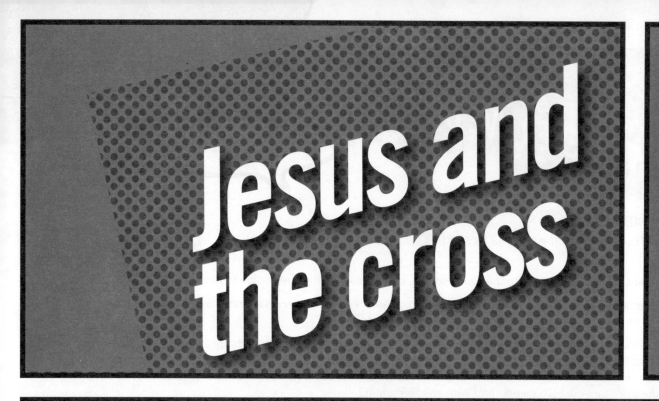

Jesus and the cross

THE STORY OF EASTER IS CENTRAL TO THE CHRISTIAN FAITH. JESUS' ACTIONS CHANGED THE WORLD AND STILL HAVE AN IMPACT ON LIVES TODAY. HIS DEFEAT OF DEATH, HIS ACT OF RECONCILIATION, HIS TAKING THE PUNISHMENT IN OUR PLACE, HIS RESCUE MISSION – ALL OF THESE THINGS HAVE CHANGED US, AND HAVE THE POWER TO IGNITE A LOVE OF HIM IN OUR YOUNG PEOPLE. BEFORE YOU EMBARK ON THE STORIES OF THIS SECTION, THINK CAREFULLY WHAT THE EASTER NARRATIVE MEANS TO YOU. HOW DO YOU VIEW THE CROSS? YOU MIGHT FIND IT HELPFUL TO READ 'TOP TIPS ON EXPLAINING THE CROSS' (SU, 9781844273300), WHICH HELPS YOU EXPLORE THE MEANING OF THE CROSS IN FOUR DIFFERENT WAYS: JESUS THE SACRIFICE, JESUS THE RECONCILER, JESUS THE VICTOR AND JESUS THE RESCUER (OR REDEEMER).

The way you talk about the cross and what it means to you will directly influence the way your young people think about it, so make sure you have your thoughts all sorted before you approach these sessions. Don't forget that the resurrection is important too! Some young people will want to examine the evidence behind the story, and there are various books out there that will help you do that (do an online search and you'll get plenty). Others will want to know more, whilst a few won't be as positive. However, your own story (and those of your fellow leaders) will be a powerful tool – the young people will be able to see Jesus' salvation in you, an authentic example of what you are exploring together.

FOR THOSE FROM OUTSIDE A CHURCH COMMUNITY

The central message of Christianity has been lost in amongst the rather dim view that society now takes of religion. It is unlikely that young people with little or no church background have explored God's ultimate salvation plan before, so the range of responses you get may be very wide! Some may follow society's line, some may be indifferent, but some may start to understand more of what God has done for them. Sensitively question those who appear negative, while encouraging those who want to know more. This is the explosive heart of the Christian message – get ready for some fireworks!

FOR THOSE WITH A CHURCH BACKGROUND

Even among young people who you might describe as 'churched', there is a wide range of understanding of the cross and resurrection. For some it will be a side issue that sits separately from the rest of their lives; others will be interested and want to take it further. There will be those too who are on fire and want to go forward in their faith and deepen their relationship with Jesus. It is a difficult balancing act to meet the needs of all these young people, so plan carefully. You could split the group down further or provide a variety of responses.

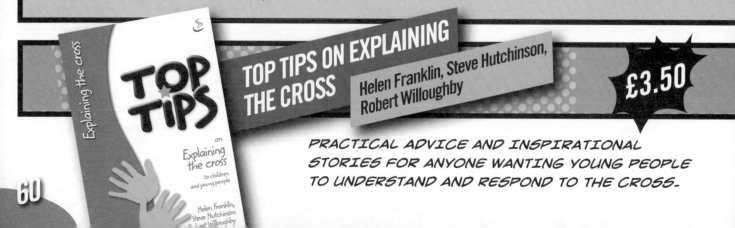

TOP TIPS ON EXPLAINING THE CROSS — Helen Franklin, Steve Hutchinson, Robert Willoughby

£3.50

PRACTICAL ADVICE AND INSPIRATIONAL STORIES FOR ANYONE WANTING YOUNG PEOPLE TO UNDERSTAND AND RESPOND TO THE CROSS.

FAME IDOL

LUKE 19:28–44

47

WHAT: *Drama*
WHY: *To answer the question 'Why follow Jesus?'*
WITH: *Copies of 'Idols' script from page 64, Bibles*

1 Look at the 'Idols' script. Pick people to read the parts, and have a dramatic read-through with the whole group. If you have time to prepare in advance, you could also stage, rehearse and perform the sketch.

2 After the sketch, say that Jesus is the King of kings and Lord of lords. Angels in heaven fall down and worship him. His disciples worship him. His followers worship him. Even the shepherds and the wise men in the Christmas story worshipped him when he was just a baby. Sadly, people around the world will fall down and worship things that are not true and have nothing to do with Jesus. These are called idols. Explain that in this sketch, we look at the question, 'What is an idol?'

3 Discuss, as a group, the types of things that people may worship or look to for help or guidance. Be aware that this could venture into a discussion on other faiths and be prepared to answer sensitively. You may like to identify that the idol in the sketch was 'self-centredness' or 'me', and guide them into thinking about more secular modern day 'idols' such as celebrity or money.

4 Then, referring back to the idea of people worshipping Jesus, ask the young people to consider the differences between Jesus and idols. Explain some of the things that had happened to Jesus before he entered Jerusalem. Jesus travelled with his disciples from Galilee to Jerusalem. Towards the end of the journey they came to Jericho where there was a blind man called Bartimaeus. Bartimaeus shouted to Jesus above everyone and asked Jesus to heal him. After Jesus had healed him, Bartimaeus followed Jesus (**Mark 10:46–52; Luke 18:35–43**). In Jericho, Jesus saw Zacchaeus, the tax collector, and invited himself to his house. Zacchaeus responded to Jesus by deciding to pay back all those people he had cheated (**Luke 19:1–10**). Bartimaeus had faith in Jesus and responded by following him (literally), whereas Zacchaeus followed Jesus by changing his behaviour and acting more like him. These events will help the young people to understand the context of Jesus' entry into Jerusalem.

5 Read **Luke 19:28–40** together; then ask why people cheered Jesus. Why did these people want to follow him?

IT IS FINISHED?

JOHN 19:17–30

48

WHAT: *Dramatic interviews*
WHY: *To learn why Jesus was crucified*
WITH: *'Dramatic interviews' from page 65*

1 Before the session, get four leaders to prepare by reading the four people stories. Ideally, you need a leader to play each of the parts in the session. If this isn't possible have leaders playing more than one part and divide the young people into the same number of groups.

2 Read **John 19:17–30**, from a modern translation, to the young people. Repeat Jesus' final words from verse 30. 'It is finished' or 'Everything is done' seem strange words. What is finished? What is the 'everything' that was done? Say that the young people are going to discover the answer to those questions by interviewing some Bible characters.

3 Divide the young people into three or four groups. Ask each group to interview the characters to see what Jesus has achieved.

4 When they have spoken to each of the four characters, bring everyone together and get the young people to give feedback.

5 Make sure they know that Jesus realised that his Father had sent him to die for the world's sins (**John 1:29**), to offer eternal life to all who turned to him (**John 3:14–17** and **6:48–58**) and to be the catalyst of the growing movement that we call the Christian faith (**John 12:23–33**). His words showed that on the cross he had completed all these tasks.

URBAN MYTH

JOHN 20:19–31

49

WHAT: *Character identification*
WHY: *To live with the belief of the resurrection*
WITH: *Copies of John 20:19–31 from a dramatised Bible, copies of the 'How sceptical are you?'*
quiz from page 66

1 Hand out copies of the quiz and ask the young people to answer the questions. Get them to share their results.

2 Give everyone a copy of **John 20:19–31** from a dramatised Bible. Either ask for four volunteers to read out the parts, or divide the young people into groups of four to read the Bible verses.

3 Ask: 'Which category do you think Thomas would have come into in the quiz?'

4 Get the young people into groups (perhaps the same ones as before). Ask them to brainstorm what the characters would have felt throughout the story. Say that the disciples had had a very special time with Jesus. They had been frightened and scared until Jesus came and greatly reassured them.

5 Invite them to focus on Thomas' feelings. Thomas would have felt left-out, jealous, possibly rejected. How would the young people have felt if everyone else had seen Jesus but them? Would they have believed them or reacted in the same way Thomas did?

6 In a time of quiet, invite the young people to think about what proof they would need to be able to call Jesus their Lord and God. What proof can they see from the world around them?

WHAT A MISSION!

MATTHEW 28:16–20

50

WHAT: *Bible study*
WHY: *To be challenged that we have a part to play in God's rescue plan*
WITH: *Copies of 'It's personal' from page 67, whiteboard or large sheet of paper, marker pens*

1 Divide the whiteboard or large sheet of paper into two columns. Write the titles 'Before Jesus' on one side and 'After Jesus' on the other.

2 Hand out copies of the 'It's personal' resource sheet and get four volunteers to read out the characters' stories. Alternatively, you could divide the young people into four groups and get each group to act out one of the stories.

3 After each story has been read or acted out, ask the group: 'What was this person like before meeting Jesus?' Write up the answers under the 'Before Jesus' heading. Then ask: 'What were they like after meeting Jesus?' Write the answers up under the 'After Jesus' heading.

4 Explain that all these stories are modern-day versions of accounts from the Bible of people who met Jesus (**Luke 19:1–10; Mark 5:1–30; John 4:1–20** and **Matthew 9:18–26**). Read out the things you have listed under 'Before Jesus' and ask: 'Are there still people like this in the world today?'

5 Get a young person to read **Matthew 28:16–20** from a contemporary version of the Bible (such as The Word on the Street). Ask everyone: 'What did Jesus command the people there (and us today) to do?'

6 Explain that Jesus has given us the most important job of all time: to share the news that Jesus can still affect people's lives just like he did in the ways listed on the 'After Jesus' list on the whiteboard. Ask the group to think and chat about how this makes them feel.

7 If appropriate, ask the young people, if they feel they have encountered, or would like to encounter, Jesus – just like the people they have been learning about did – to speak to a leader after the session.

PROMISE KEEPER

ACTS 1:1–11

WHAT: *Drama*
WHY: *To be encouraged that Jesus did not leave us alone*
WITH: *A pile of photographs, two chairs, 'Footprints revisited' from page 68, 'Footprints' poem (optional)*

1 Invite two young people to act out the 'Footprints revisited' script. (You could ask them to rehearse this before the session.)

2 If you have it, ask someone to read out the poem 'Footprints'.

3 Ask the young people to think about a period in their life when they had a hard time, like the ones Joe thought of. Invite them to talk about the experience with a partner.

4 Encourage them to feed back their answers to the whole group if they wish.

5 Read **Acts 1:1–11**. Explain to the young people that, just like Joe, Jesus' disciples probably felt abandoned and alone. However, by receiving the Holy Spirit the disciples could trust that God would always be with them.

Idols

by Marco Palmer

THE CHARACTERS

HONEST LOU= DEVIOUS SALESMAN)

CHIEF WALLA WALLA BING BANG= CHIEF OF VILLAGE

MISS MU

MIRROR

Scene: Honest Lou shouts to the crowds in the open air market.

HONEST LOU= Idols! Graven images! Step up and get your idols! They're cute! They're cuddly! Take one home to ya missus! Buy one for ya grandma! Hey! Is there an all-powerful deity interfering with your gaiety? Then try my easy solution without painful absolution. No mess! No fuss! It's me you can trust! Give your old god the boot! Let me find a substitute. My name is Honest Lou, and I'll find the ideal idol deal for you!

(Chief Walla Walla Bing Bang enters.)

HONEST LOU= *(To audience.)* Excuse me, ladies and gentlemen, an old friend of mine just dropped by. Be with you in a moment. *(To Chief.)* Chief Walla Walla Bing Bang, what seems to be the problem this time?

CHIEF= *(Yells in angry jungle jibberish.)* Oo ee oo aa aa! Oo ee oo aa aa!

HONEST LOU= You're afraid of your idols!

CHIEF= *(Yells in angry jungle jibberish, cowers and bows repeatedly.)* Oo ee oo aa aa! Oo ee oo aa aa!

HONEST LOU= I understand! I understand! The great mother-in-law idol, Mamamba-Mamba-Nagga-Nagga is indeed fierce and needs to be appeased.

CHIEF= *(Angrily.)* Oo ee oo aa aa! Oo ee oo aa aa!

HONEST LOU= So did you try the great appeasement festival of sacrificing the best of your crops, your goats and your chickens to the great Mamamba-Mamba-Nagga-Nagga? She still won't make it rain?

CHIEF= *(Angrily.)* Oo ee oo aa aa! Oo ee oo aa aa!

HONEST LOU= Did you try dancing for your idol?

CHIEF= *(Dances around.)* Oo ee oo aa aa! Oo ee oo aa aa!

HONEST LOU= That's pathetic! Pathetic! You've got to put more feeling into it, Chief. More feeling!

CHIEF= *(Sings.)* Oo ee oo aa aa! Oo ee oo aa aa!

HONEST LOU= No! No! No! No! I think the only thing that will satisfy and appease the great Mamamba-Mamba-Nagga-Nagga is the sacrifice of some sons-in-law!

CHIEF= *(On knees, begging for mercy.)* Oo ee oo aa aa! Oo ee oo aa aa!

HONEST LOU= Oh alright! I will let you trade your idol in for one you are less afraid of. Why don't you worship the great fertiliser god, the great Da-Dunga-Dunga?

CHIEF= Da-Dunga-Dunga?

HONEST LOU= You'll have hours of fun holding your breath and worshipping the great Da-Dunga-Dunga! It captures the real essence of all idols. Now why don't you run back to your tribe and teach them the Da-Dunga-Dunga dance?

(Chief Walla Walla Bing Bang dances off stage.)

HONEST LOU= *(To audience.)* Well, there goes another happy, satisfied customer. What are you waiting for?! *(Miss Mu enters.)* Miss Mu, how are you? Will you bow down to our idol and take it home with you? It outsells every other idol. Mirror, come on out here! *(Mirror enters, singing the Carly Simon song 'You're so vain!')*

MIRROR= You're so vain! You probably think this song is about you! Don't you? Don't you?

HONEST LOU= Well, my dear, I bet you're thinking, 'Why, that's just...'

MIRROR= I'm no mere mirror... get it? Mere mirror... oh, never mind.

HONEST LOU= My dear, talk to it! Say, 'Mirror, mirror, off the wall, who is the fairest of them all?'

(Miss Mu repeats these words as she looks at the Mirror. The Mirror mimics every movement she makes.)

MISS MU= Mirror, Mirror, off the wall, who is the fairest of them all?

MIRROR: Who is the fairest of them all? Why, it's you! Your happiness and comfort come before anything else. Your freedom and rights outweigh the freedom and rights of any other human being. Baby, you are the centre of the universe; your every whim and desire must be met! Oh, just look in the mirror and bow down and worship! Shout 'Halelu-meeeee!' Hey, girl! You don't really want to give yourself over to any god. God's gonna ask you to do a lot of things you just don't want to do: like look after others, love and forgive other people, put other people before yourself, and put God first! You're gonna have to give your life away, your time away, your money! Why don't you give in to selfishness? Why don't you bow down to me?

HONEST LOU: So, my dear, what do you say? Will you bow down to this idol and take it home with you today?

MISS MU: No!

MIRROR: What?! Look what you're doing to me! *(Sinks to knees like the Wicked Witch of the West.)* You're killing me! *(Flops over and dies.)*

HONEST LOU: Look what you did! You killed my best idol! (Reluctantly, Lou yells.) Well, I am disappointed in you! You set your mind fully on things above! That's terrible.

MIRROR: Oh relax, Lou. I'll be back tomorrow!

HONEST LOU: And so will I!

DRAMATIC INTERVIEWS

CHARACTER 1: A DISCIPLE OF JOHN THE BAPTIST

(John 1:29)

I heard John the Baptist say of Jesus, 'Here is the Lamb of God who takes away the sin of the world.' That title reminds me of so much. When the Israelites were trying to leave Egypt they were told to slaughter a lamb and put its blood around the door to protect their family from the Angel of Death. Also a lamb was slaughtered at the Temple each morning and evening because of the sins of the people. And then there are the words of the prophets. Jeremiah and Isaiah both spoke of the chosen one who would be led to death like a lamb to the slaughter.

CHARACTER 2: NICODEMUS THE PHARISEE

(John 3:14–17)

When I was talking to Jesus, he called himself the Son of Man and said that he would be lifted up like the metal snake that Moses lifted up in the desert. When the Israelites were in the wilderness, having escaped from Egypt, a plague of poisonous snakes attacked them. God told Moses to make a snake of bronze and to hold it up. Anyone who looked on it would not die.

CHARACTER 3: ONE OF JESUS' FOLLOWERS

(John 6:48–58)

Jesus told us he was the Bread of Life. He compared himself to the manna that God sent to the Israelites when they were in the wilderness after escaping from Egypt. He explained that the manna did not make them live for ever, but he would.

CHARACTER 4: A PERSON IN THE CROWD
(John 12:23-33)

Jesus called himself the Son of Man and told us that a grain of wheat must fall to the ground and die if it is to produce lots of wheat. He also told us that he would have to be lifted up from the earth.

How sceptical are you?

Do you always believe what you are told? Does it depend on who told you? Try this quiz to see how sceptical you are.

 1 YOUR TEACHER TELLS YOU THAT THE WORLD IS FLAT. DO YOU...

a) believe them – teachers know everything
b) ask for proof
c) convince them that you know better – on your last trip on the Starship Enterprise you took some pictures, 'Here, have a look'?

 2 YOUR FRIEND TELLS YOU THAT SHE HAD PURPLE KETCHUP FOR TEA. DO YOU...

a) believe her – it sounds bizarre but she wouldn't lie
b) buy some chips and then ask for some ketchup and see what she produces
c) ask her where she got it from, how much it was and what additives they use to get from the normal red colour of tomatoes?

 3 YOUR FRIEND TELLS YOU AN AMAZING STORY OF A MAN, WHO WAS DEAD, BEING ALIVE AGAIN. DO YOU...

a) believe them
b) ask to see the death certificate and then ask to pop round to the person's house for some tea, with a portion of chips and purple ketchup
c) ask what the person died from, how long they were dead and then ask to see the doctor who can verify that the person is truly alive?

HOW DID YOU DO?

MOSTLY As
You're a very trusting individual. You always seem to believe people without question. Be wary of believing everything you're told – ask more questions.

MOSTLY Bs
You need lots of convincing and hard evidence to believe anything. Do you always have to see something to believe it? What other ways can you use to convince you?

MOSTLY Cs
You like to assess the situation, ask lots of questions then decide what you believe. Congratulations! You're on the right track.

What were each of these people like before they met Jesus? What changed?

SCAM UNCOVERED IN LOCAL SHOP

I work in a busy local shop. I've got the greatest scam going – I overcharge everyone! So, if someone's bill comes to £20, I charge them £30. And the extra £10 goes in my pocket! I've made so much money! The word is that some people know my game and hate my guts, but I don't care. Why should I? I'm looking after number one.

AND THEN...

It amazed everyone that Jesus chose to see me. Lots of things have changed since I met Jesus. I still work in the shop, but I don't overcharge people anymore. In fact, sometimes I undercharge them! I guess it's my way of making up for what I took. I sold my car and used the money to pay back the people I'd overcharged. I reckon it's the least I can do.

CRAZY PARANOID PETE

I was quite young when my problems began. It was like I was being tortured inside. I couldn't remember what it was like to feel peaceful or calm. Everywhere I went, I was convinced people were saying bad things about me. Sometimes the only way to release all the bad feelings was to scream. People thought I was crazy and maybe I was. No one would do anything to help me. I ended up living on the streets and was the laughing-stock of the town.

AND THEN...

After I met Jesus everything changed. The terrible feelings went. The paranoia went. It was like I had got my life back. No more shouting either. I got myself some decent clothes and cleaned myself up. It was like all the bad stuff in me had been washed off. No one in the town can believe I'm the same person as before. All I know is I feel great and I hope it stays like this.

ASYLUM SEEKER TRUTH

I'm a refugee from a war-torn country. I came here because I'd been threatened by the government back home. I don't talk about it and know one here knows about it. I've been given a one-bedroom flat in a nice area but the people here hate me. I get called names, I had a brick thrown through my window, and I had 'Go home!' graffitied on my front door. Don't get me wrong, I've not led a perfect life, but I certainly don't deserve any of this.

AND THEN...

I couldn't believe Jesus would talk to me. I was at the bus stop when he came up and started chatting. I was shocked; no one talks to me – unless it's to shout abuse. But Jesus didn't do that. He wanted to talk to me. He told me stuff about me that no one else knows. He knew about all the stuff I'd done wrong too, but he didn't condemn me. I know he was someone special – who else could know all that stuff? He told me to go to the local community centre and tell everyone there about our conversation. So that's what I did. I've never met anyone like him before.

DEAD DAUGHTER DELIGHT

Our daughter, Natalie, had been ill since she was a baby. She was 8 years old when things took a turn for the worse. The hospitals in the UK had done everything they could for her, but nothing worked. My husband and I found out about a new treatment in America – it was our last hope. Everyone in America was sure she'd be OK. But after only two weeks back in the UK, Natalie got worse. She was rushed to hospital but there was nothing they could do and she died. We were devastated.

AND THEN...

I can't explain how Jesus did it, but he did. One minute Natalie was lying in that terrible mortuary, the next she came running out to us. I didn't know whether to laugh, cry or faint. Natalie was alive and all signs of the illness had gone. The doctors simply could not understand it. They said it was a 'miracle'. A few days later we had a fantastic welcome home party for her, and all her friends came along. Now she is back at school, playing with her friends like nothing ever happened.

CHECK OUT THE ORIGINAL VERSIONS IN LUKE 19:1–10, MARK 5:1–20, JOHN 4:1–30 AND MATTHEW 9:18–26.

'Footprints' revisited

THE CHARACTERS
·······································
JOE, GOD

Scene: Joe is sitting on a chair reading his Bible. There's an empty chair next to him.

(God enters, holding pile or album of photographs, and sits down on the chair.)

GOD: Hi, Joe! How's it going?

JOE: Hey, God. I was just reading some of this book you lent me. Who would have thought that a book with the title 'The Bible' would be an international bestseller?! There aren't even any pictures in here. But so far, it's a pretty exciting story. The bit about the guy who got swallowed by a fish was crazy!

GOD: Yeah, that's one of my favourites. Jonah wouldn't eat fishfingers for a whole year after that incident.

JOE: I can't really blame the guy. He must have smelled horrible after sitting in fish guts for three days! But hey, everything turned out alright in the end, and he learned a lot on the journey.

GOD: That's very true. I'm glad you see it that way. And speaking of journeys, I've been taking some snapshots of your life's journey over the past few decades and I thought you might like to take a look.

JOE: Wow, I'd love to!

(God takes out the photos and hands them to Joe. Joe starts flipping through them – his facial expression should quickly turn to confusion.)

JOE: These are just pictures of footprints during various points in my life.

GOD: That's right. Those footprints are yours and mine. See, there they are on the day you were born, and when you won your first relay race at school, and there they are during your tenth birthday party.

JOE: Was that the one when I ate too much cake and was sick all over my friend's trainers?

GOD: No, that was your ninth birthday party.

JOE: Oh yeah. I remember now. Why didn't you stop me from eating all that cake?

GOD: Free will, Joe. I didn't stop Eve from eating that piece of fruit, did I?

JOE: Fair enough!

(Joe flips through a few more pictures.)

GOD: And this picture was taken the day your dog died... and that one was taken when you found out you failed your maths exam ... and this one is from the week when you thought your mum might have cancer.

JOE: Hey, wait a minute ... where did the other set of footprints go? During all the best parts of my life, there are always two sets of footprints. And during all the worst bits, when I was miserable and I needed you most, there's only one set! How could you just leave me like that?!

GOD: Joe, my son, you know I love you and I would never leave you. During the worst times in your life, when you were really suffering, you only see one set of footprints because it was then that I carried you.

JOE: Really? Wow. I guess I should have known that. You've always been there for me when I needed you. Sorry for doubting you.

GOD: That's alright. You're not the first to feel that way. Jonah felt pretty down during those three days in the big fish. He was certain that I'd left him to swim around in fish food for ever. But I was with him all the way. There are lots of other people who were certain I'd abandoned them during the rough times – Job and David, to name a few. You know, next time you're reading my book, flip ahead to **Acts 1:1–11**. I think you might be able to relate to how the disciples must have felt when they thought Jesus might abandon them.

JOE: OK, thanks, I will! I always thought everyone in the Bible had it figured out and never struggled the way I do. But I guess I was wrong about that too.

GOD: The thing to remember, Joe, is that I'm always here. In the good times and the bad. And no matter how many times you mess up or doubt or struggle, I still love you.

JOE: Thanks, God. From now on I'm not going to get so worried about things – because I know you'll carry me through.

(Based on 'Footprints', a poem written by Mary Stevenson)

The early church

THE CHURCH TODAY DOESN'T DO ITSELF ANY FAVOURS IN TERMS OF MARKETING AND PR. ASK A YOUNG PERSON WHO HAS LITTLE EXPERIENCE OF CHURCH WHAT THEY THINK OF GOD'S PEOPLE MEETING TOGETHER AND YOU'LL GET A GOOD IDEA WHY. YOUNG PEOPLE MIGHT DESCRIBE IT AS BORING, IRRELEVANT, FOR OLD PEOPLE. AND WHATEVER WE THINK OF CHURCH, WE'RE NOT GETTING THE RIGHT MESSAGE ACROSS.

But the early church wasn't like this. It was a dangerous and exciting place to be. The coming of the Holy Spirit unleashed God's great power on Jesus' followers. People were attracted to this life-changing message and, every day, more joined the group of believers. Miracles were seen (often very unusual ones – check out Acts 5:12–16 for a start!) and God's power was shown in many ways through this body of believers.

Before you embark on any of these sessions with young people, think about your own reactions to these passages. How similar are you to those early believers? Are you all out in the same way they were, or do you have reservations about some things? Are some areas of your life out of bounds to the Holy Spirit? Don't beat yourself up about things, but open yourself up to what God could do in you. This is not about doing more and running yourself ragged. It's about listening to God and going after what he wants for us.

FOR THOSE FROM OUTSIDE A CHURCH COMMUNITY

The Holy Spirit is an unusual person to explore with young people from outside a church community. Ideas of God the Father and Jesus are much easier to grasp. The fact that many Christians disagree about the role of the Spirit makes things even more difficult. As you explore Pentecost and the other passages here, be mindful of your church's view of the Spirit and also where the young people are culturally. It can be easy for young people to get the wrong impression, so approach these sessions prayerfully and carefully.

FOR THOSE WITH A CHURCH BACKGROUND

These sessions look at the start of the church and what the Holy Spirit did when he was sent by the Father. Take time with church young people to look at the differences between what God was doing then and what God is doing in the church now. Where do they see God at work in their church and in the church in general? Encourage them to see where they can play a part – how can they exercise their gifts to serve others in their congregation? Where can they be part of a church looking to God and doing his work?

TRANSFORMED

ACTS 2:1–4,
33–47

52

WHAT: *Challenges*
WHY: *To recognise some of the ways the Holy Spirit was at work among the first Christians*
WITH *A copy of the two challenges from page 72 for each small group*

1 Get everyone into small groups of three or four young people and give each group a copy of these two challenges:

- *Challenge 1:* a foolproof way of communicating a message to every person in the whole world
- *Challenge 2:* a foolproof way of getting everyone to change their lives in response to what they have heard

They will need to work together on the challenges. How could they achieve these two things? What tools would they use?

2 Ask for feedback from the groups. Be positive about any creative solutions.

3 Say that God had similar challenges. Encourage the group to listen for how God achieved his challenges with the first Christians. He needed:

Challenge 1: a way of communicating the message of the good news of Jesus to the whole world.
Solution: Jesus' followers were sitting in a room when the Holy Spirit showed up spectacularly.
Bible verses to read: **Acts 2:1–4**
Question: What would be the best way to describe the work of the Holy Spirit in this event?

Challenge 2: a way of enabling people to change their lives radically because of what they'd heard.
Solution: The giving of the Holy Spirit to all the disciples.
Bible verse to read: **Acts 2:33** (last sentence), **38, 39, 43–47**
Question: What would be the best way to describe the work of the Holy Spirit in this event?

PAUL SEES THE LIGHT

ACTS 9:1–19A

53

WHAT: *Drama and questions*
WHY: *To explore God's plan to spread the good news*
WITH: *Copies of the drama challenge from page 72*

1 Divide the young people into groups of about six, if necessary. Give each group a copy of the drama challenge.

2 Explain that they have a few minutes to put together a drama based on the information they've been given. Everyone must play some part in the drama. Encourage the young people to be as creative as they can in preparing their dramas and allow them to use any extra props that they can think of.

3 Bring the young people together and get each group to act out their drama. Ask the following questions:
- What sort of people do you think Saul used to hang around with? (**Acts 8:1–4**)
- Would this experience affect who his friends were? Why?
- If Saul's job was to get rid of all the Christians, what effect would his experience have on his job?
- How do you think people would have reacted to Saul's conversion – both the Jewish people and the Christians?
- If you were to have a huge experience of God, like Saul, what difference do you think it would make to your life?
- Do you think your current experience of God or what you know about him affects or changes your life in any way? If so, in what ways and why?

4 Conclude by saying that Saul's experience of God led to a radical change of life. Although many people don't experience God in the same way as Saul, if we truly are following God, it should make some difference to our lives.

BARNABAS SORTS IT OUT

ACTS 9:19B–31

54

WHAT: Collage
WHY: To explore God's plan to spread the good news
WITH: Magazines and newspapers, paper, pens, scissors, glue

1. Divide the young people into groups of three or four and give each group a selection of magazines and newspapers.

2. Encourage the groups to choose a celebrity and create a collage showing them doing an unlikely job. For example, David Beckham doing ballet.

3. Bring everyone together and encourage the young people to show their collage and explain what it is. Discuss what is unlikely about each of them and decide which is the most ridiculous or unbelievable.

4. Read **Acts 9:19b–31** to the young people. Say that this is how the disciples felt when they heard that Saul was preaching about Jesus. It was ridiculous – unbelievable. Surely it was a trick, or a joke? But it turned out to be true. God can make changes in people which we cannot imagine, as part of his plan to spread the good news.

EVERYONE SAYS YES

ACTS 15:1–35

55

WHAT: Role play
WHY: To explore God's plan to spread the good news
WITH: Bibles

1. Read **Acts 15:1–35** aloud to the young people, or get a confident young person to read it.

2. In groups, give the young people ten minutes to create their own modern-day drama or role play based on the passage. If they are struggling for ideas, suggest these as possible settings to get them started:

   A new boy starts at your school. He wants to hang out with you and your mates, and although you are keen for him to join in, your mates are not so sure… How do you convince them?

   You have new neighbours, and their daughter is your age and interested in jazz dance, like you. You'd love to get to know her, but your friends would think her dress sense was so uncool. What do you do?

   Your friend's brother wants to join the football team. You know he's an excellent striker, but his attitude to training is very different, and the rest of the team might need some convincing. Should you encourage him to join the team?

3. Invite the groups to present their dramas or role plays.

4. Chat through the following questions with the young people:

   Why did you end the dramas or role plays the way you did?

   How did you manage to convince the others to let the person join your crowd?

   Was that the right thing to do, and why?

   What does this say about God's plan to spread the good news? How does the drama reflect God's plan to spread the good news, as shown in the passage? (How is the drama the same, and how is it different?)

Challenge Cards

CHALLENGE 1

A FOOLPROOF WAY OF COMMUNICATING A MESSAGE TO EVERY PERSON IN THE WHOLE WORLD

CHALLENGE 2

A FOOLPROOF WAY OF GETTING EVERYONE TO CHANGE THEIR LIVES IN RESPONSE TO WHAT THEY HAVE HEARD

DRAMA CHALLENGE

Your challenge is to act out the most creative drama possible based on the information below. You could mime the drama, do a *High School Musical* version, use props, make up a rap or something completely different. The more creative you can be the better. Everyone in your group must take part in your drama and you must cover all of these points:

- SAUL'S JOB IS TO PERSECUTE CHRISTIANS — KILLING THEM OR PUTTING THEM INTO JAIL.

- ONE DAY, AS SAUL IS WALKING FROM ONE TOWN TO ANOTHER, HE IS BLINDED BY A BRIGHT LIGHT; HE HEARS A VOICE WHO SAYS HE IS JESUS, ASKING HIM WHY HE IS BEING SO CRUEL TO HIM. THE PEOPLE WITH SAUL WITNESS THE EVENTS BUT CAN'T SEE WHO IS SPEAKING TO SAUL.

- WHEN THE BRIGHT LIGHT GOES, SAUL IS BLINDED. SO HIS FRIENDS LEAD HIM TO THE ADDRESS OF WHERE THE VOICE TOLD HIM TO GO.

- MEANWHILE, GOD SPEAKS TO A BLOKE CALLED ANANIAS, WHO IS A FOLLOWER OF JESUS. GOD TELLS HIM THAT SAUL IS ON HIS WAY AND THAT HE SHOULD PUT HIS HANDS ON HIM TO HEAL HIS BLINDNESS.

- ANANIAS IS TERRIFIED AS HE KNOWS SAUL USUALLY KILLS CHRISTIANS. HOWEVER, HE DECIDES TO TRUST AND OBEY GOD.

- SAUL TURNS UP AND ANANIAS DOES WHAT HE IS TOLD. STRAIGHTAWAY SAUL CAN SEE. SAUL BECOMES A FOLLOWER OF JESUS.

Living the life

THIS FINAL SECTION LOOKS AT SOME PASSAGES FROM THE EPISTLES AND REVELATION. IF CHRIST HAS DIED FOR US, WHAT DOES THAT MEAN? HOW SHOULD WE LIVE AS PEOPLE OF GOD? WILL LIFE BE EASY IF WE ACCEPT JESUS? AS YOUNG PEOPLE LEARN MORE ABOUT GOD, REGARDLESS OF THEIR BACKGROUND, THEY WILL START TO ASK THESE QUESTIONS. IF THEY ACCEPT CHRIST, THEN THEIR LIFE WILL CHANGE AND THESE PASSAGES GIVE SOME GREAT GUIDANCE FOR THOSE FIRST STEPS.

These passages are full of amazing imagery – the body, running a race, a soldier's armour, a supernatural vision of Christ and Jesus' triumphal return. In a culture where visual media is a key part in communication, these pictures can be as powerful today as they were when they were written. Many young people learn visually, so make the most of these visual opportunities.

Take some time to familiarise yourself with these passages. You may have read them all before, but try to read them as if it were the first time you had encountered them. What things stand out? What issues are raised? 1 Corinthians 12 calls us to work in harmony, rather than being jealous or self-aggrandising. Hebrews reminds us that this is not a sprint – an unusual message in today's 'now' culture. The armour of God puts forward the image that we're in a battle – what does that mean for us? Finally, the images of Jesus at the end of time bring some glorious thoughts but perhaps some more disturbing ones too.

FOR THOSE FROM OUTSIDE A CHURCH COMMUNITY
Make full use of the imagery here to help young people with little or no church background to access the ideas being expressed. Many of these passages go against prevailing truths in today's culture. It's not 'me first' with God. We won't get everything all at once and be able to relax. Things won't be easy for us. And at the end, we have to be ready and we will be called to account. Don't shy away from these challenges, but let the young people wrestle with them head on. You may be surprised how much the Spirit leads the young people to discover for themselves!

FOR THOSE WITH A CHURCH BACKGROUND
The challenge is relevant for those from within the church as well as those from outside. It may be that they have not really thought about the way they live their life as a Christian. For many church young people, Christianity is held in tension with the other areas of their life, and is often held separately. These passages will help them understand that they are part of something bigger and that Jesus' call affects their whole life, not just on a Sunday morning.

BODY BEAUTIFUL

1 CORINTHIANS 12:14–27

 56

WHAT: Drama and Bible study
WHY: To explore what it means for the church to be the body of Christ
WITH: Bibles, copies of 'On strike!' script from page 77

1 Read **1 Corinthians 12:14–21,26,27** to the group.

2 Ask the group to imagine what might happen if one part of their body decided to go on strike.

3 Get five people to read the script 'On strike!' and perform it now. (They could have rehearsed this beforehand.)

4 Ask the young people if anyone has had to manage without a part of the body that they normally take for granted – for example, if they have broken an arm, or had their mouth frozen at the dentist's. Ask: 'What was it like?'

5 Ask: What does verse 27 mean? Where is Jesus now? Explain that he returned to heaven, but that Paul is saying that the church is his body here on earth. Each Christian has an important part to play.

STARTERS' ORDERS

HEBREWS 11:39 – 12:3

 57

WHAT: Wacky race
WHY: To understand that the Christian life is an ongoing race
WITH: A blindfold, large-sized heavy boots, a long scarf, a plastic jug of water

1 Mark out a short race distance with start and finish lines. Choose four volunteers to compete in the 'Wacky race'. Say that they must get to the finish line first to win. Get everyone else lined up to cheer them on.

2 Line up the contestants at the start. Blindfold the first contestant, make the second contestant wear the large boots, tie the scarf around the knees of the third contestant and get the fourth to balance the jug of water on the back of their hand.

3 As you give out the 'handicaps', say to each person, 'You may not remove this until the end of the race.' Start the race and cheer on the competitors.

4 Repeat the race with four new volunteers. Whisper to them that although they must not remove their own 'handicaps', there is no rule against removing each other's.

5 Discuss with the young people the difference that the help of others made to the runners. Read **Hebrews 11:39 – 12:3** to the group.

6 Explain that being a Christian is like being in a race. And we've seen that the race is easier with help.

7 Get the young people to think about this: Jesus taught that we should love one another as we love ourselves (**Matthew 22:39**) – helping each other is one way to show this. What could you do to help others in your life?

TOOLED UP

EPHESIANS 6:10–18

58

WHAT: *Quiz and reflection*
WHY: *To recognise that God prepares us for the battle ahead in the Christian life*
WITH: *Bibles or copies of Ephesians 6:10–18, a bag of props: a shoe, a hat, a belt, a shield, a toy sword, a breastplate (eg, waistcoat, flak jacket). (Alternatively, find images of these items.)*

1 Ask the group if they have ever forgotten something really important when they have been out for the day, at school or on holiday. Suggest that they tell the person next to them what they forgot and what happened as a result.

2 Say that packing the right stuff for where you are going is important. Give out Bibles or copies of the Bible passage (if the young people are not used to Bibles). Ask for a couple of volunteers to read **Ephesians 6:10–1**8, and remind the young people to follow the text as it is being read.

3 Bring out the bag of props (or pictures). Ask for a volunteer to pick something out of the bag and challenge everyone to find where that item of armour is mentioned in the passage. Ask: 'Why do you think that item might be important?' Repeat until all items have been selected.

4 Explain that through God we can have all these things to live our lives, especially when it's tough, but also when things are going fine. To live to the fullest as Christians we need to make sure we are prepared. The armour of God is a great illustration of how we should prepare ourselves.

I'LL BE BACK

1 THESSALONIANS 4:13 – 5:11

59

WHAT: *Drama and group discussion*
WHY: *To be encouraged that Jesus is on his way back*
WITH: *'At the Chinese restaurant' script from page 78, Bible, props (two plates, two pairs of chopsticks, two fortune cookies or biscuits – optional)*

1 Before the session, arrange for two people to rehearse the 'At the Chinese restaurant' drama.

2 Get these two people to perform the drama, or alternatively let the young people read it for themselves.

3 Explain that the note which the second diner was reading came from the Bible: **1 Thessalonians 4:13 – 5:11**. Read the verses to the group from your Bible. Ask, 'What does this mean for the world?' Yes, there will be destruction, but it means an end to the world as we know it. It also means the end of man-made and natural disasters – no more murders, famines, wars, etc.

4 Ask the group, 'How do the verses make you feel? Excited, worried, fearful? Why?' It is possible that some of the young people will feel that they haven't made the grade so the verses could be quite scary for them. Remind them what the second diner said about being able to do something about it and read **1 Thessalonians 5:9,10** to the group. Say that God has provided the way out.

5 Explain that God doesn't want us to be worried or scared about the future so he reminds us of what he has done for us in the past. We should not commit our lives to him because we fear the future, but because we are grateful for what he has already done for us when he gave Jesus to die for us. He wants us to live in the present, responding to the past and eagerly anticipating the future.

6 Offer everyone the opportunity of talking more on a one-to-one basis after your session.

GLORY IS SO NOW

REVELATION 1

WHAT: *Create a newspaper*
WHY: *To recognise that Jesus is in heaven but his word is still with us*
WITH: *Large sheets of paper and marker pens*

1 Tell the group that they are going to be top reporters and newspaper editors, creating the front page of several newspapers.

2 Divide the group into pairs or threes and let them decide what sort of newspaper they are creating. Is it a tabloid, or a serious broadsheet type, or something in between? They are going to hear a lot of information about someone who (it is reported) has been saying amazing things about a man called Jesus. This 'someone' is called John.

3 Get a leader to pretend to be John and read all of **Revelation 1**. The leader needs to be as animated as possible! If you have time, arrange for someone to retell the events outlined in these Bible verses, possibly dressing up as someone from New Testament times. As they listen, encourage the young people to make notes.

4 Give the groups time to make their front pages. On large sheets of paper they need to create a mock-up of their front pages with headlines, reports and other stories that in some way relate to the Bible verses they have just heard. If they ask, allow them to use Bibles for reference.

5 Bring the young people back together and invite them to show the front page of their newspaper. You may be able to draw out some common themes or headings from among them all.

6 Explain that John had a vision and he was so excited by it he had to share it. They shouldn't worry if not all of it makes sense. John goes on to say some pretty strange things and, to be honest, Christians can't agree on exactly what it means. But John said some great things about Jesus. He said that he was in heaven in glory but, as you can see from the words written in the Bible, he is also with us, today, by the Holy Spirit – we can hear him speak to us through the Bible and talk to him in prayer.

7 Get everyone to look at all the headlines again. Read **Revelation 1:5,6** again. End with a prayer thanking Jesus for all he was while he lived on earth, all he still is in heaven and, as we have seen in this session, how he still speaks to us through the Bible.

On strike!

THE CHARACTERS
....

BRAIN, NOSE, MOUTH, HAND, EYES.
BUT YOU NEED TO IMAGINE THAT ALL
THE BODY PARTS ARE THERE.

BRAIN: Well, guys, we're nearly at the end of our weekly management meeting. We've discussed what we're going to do if Herbert eats cabbage again – Stomach will take the lead on that one. We're agreed that only Arm and Hand will move when the alarm goes off tomorrow morning – to hit the snooze button. So now we're onto 'Any Other Business'. Nose, I believe you had something that you wanted to say?

NOSE: Yes – I'm going on strike as of tomorrow morning. I have been so overworked this last week because of this cold that Herbert has had. Twenty-seven times I got blown yesterday, and my edges are getting all sore and red. I look ridiculous. So I'm going to block myself up and go on strike – no breathing, no smelling, no running and definitely no being blown.

EYES: So we'll be able to do the old joke: 'Herbert's got no nose! How does he smell? Terrible!' Hee hee!

MOUTH: Eyes, trust you to treat it as a big joke. Nose, you are being ridiculous. It's not just you that has been affected by this cold. I've been coughing every night and Lungs has been sending up some disgusting green stuff that I've had to spit out or dispatch down to Stomach. If you go on strike, I'll have to work even harder by doing all the breathing. You are so selfish. Brain, if Nose goes on strike, I want double pay.

HAND: I agree that this cold has affected us all. I've been involved in all the nose-blowing too, and have had to dispose of zillions of tissues. Nose, if you go on strike, Mouth will get dried up in the night so we won't get much sleep and I'll be the one who has to move glasses of water around in the dark so Herbert can have a drink – that's skilful work, that is.

MOUTH: Are you saying that I don't do my job properly? Flipping cheek! You just don't want Nose to go on strike because then you won't be able to pick him. I'm thinking of the well-being of all of us. If Nose stops working, then we won't be able to taste anything – Taste Buds will be out of a job, Throat will feel unappreciated, Stomach will start complaining … it will be chaos!

HAND: Fancy saying that Herbert picks his nose! He hasn't done that since primary school.

MOUTH: Oh yes he does, and I can prove it. There's lots of you involved in that disgusting habit. Well, if Nose goes on strike, then I'm going on strike as well.

EYES: You can't do that – how is Herbert going to breathe? And if he can't breathe we are all doomed! You're being selfish now.

MOUTH: If I'm really that indispensable then I definitely should get a pay rise. I demand more regular teeth cleaning, apricot flavoured lip balm and minty fresh mouthwash.

HAND: Well, all those create more work for me, so I want extra pay.

MOUTH: We don't need you. We'll just get your brother to do all the work.

HAND: How can you say that you don't need me! I've never been so insulted in all my life. That's it – I'm going on strike too!

(Body parts all start arguing amongst themselves.)

BRAIN: Head! Shoulders, stop that! Knees, and Toes! Knees, and Toes – I'm warning you. Look, guys, we mustn't argue. The truth is that none of us can operate on our own. We all have to muck in during a crisis like this cold. And as I'm the one that controls all of you lot, no one can go on strike without me saying so anyway. So behave or I'll make Herbert go and visit his Aunty Doris and you know what that means – hair combed, uncomfortable clothes, sloppy kisses on the cheeks, horrible beetroot sandwiches, everyone on our best behaviour and hours of mind-numbingly boring stories about the War. You have been warned!

ALL: *(Desperate to avoid a visit to Aunty Doris.)* OK, boss!

At the Chinese restaurant

Scene: a couple are sitting at the table of a Chinese restaurant, having just finished their meal.

ONE: *(Pushes his plate away from him, leans back and rubs his full stomach.)* Well, that was a great Chinese meal.

TWO: Sure was! They really know how to do a mean Cha-Shao Quick-Roast Beef.

ONE: The omelette and chips were good too.

TWO: *(Looking at One rather disapprovingly.)* Yeah.

ONE: Just the fortune cookies to open then.

TWO: If we must.

(One and Two crack open their cookies. One finds a small note in his and then turns his attention to Two who is unfolding a large piece of paper – actually **1 Thessalonians 4:1 – 5:11**.*)*

ONE: *(Reading his note, trying not to show his disappointment.)* 'To follow the bottle-nose dolphin, you must launch your boat into the waters.' Hmm, I wonder what that means.

TWO: Perhaps you're going on a Caribbean cruise.

ONE: *(Excitedly.)* Do you think so?

TWO: No.

ONE: Oh, you were just joking! Anyway, what does your cookie say?

(Two starts to read it to herself quietly, mumbling the occasional word.)

ONE: No, no! Read it out. I want to hear if you're joining me in the Caribbean.

TWO: Well, it tells me that one day I'm going to be with God in heaven, that there'll be all the usual things – you know, trumpet blasts, archangels and the like. And then Jesus will return and take me to his Father.

ONE: Cor, when's that going to happen?

TWO: Well, it says that no one knows. It will happen totally out of the blue and catch many people unawares, but it will happen – that's for sure.

ONE: How come you get all that and I just get this note about a dolphin?

TWO: I suppose because I follow Christ. You see, this note is from the Bible. It says that because all those who believe and trust in Jesus will be taken by him to be with God. That's a 100% guarantee.

ONE: *(Blowing his cheeks out.)* I need some of that, don't I? I don't want a dolphin... or a cruise.

TWO: *(Pleased at her friend's response.)* That's right, and you can do something about it.

ONE: Yeah, and I know what to do. *(He turns around and clicks his finger in the air.)* Waiter, this cookie's faulty. Can you bring me another one?

(Two shakes her head, closing her eyes and then putting her head in her hands.)